Praise for *Your (Re)Defining Moments*

"Each of us has been created for the purpose of fitting into a divine mosaic that works in perfect harmony with everyone and everything else, and the next major expansion of consciousness on this planet will inevitably occur when we as individuals embrace our own nature and begin working with each other and the physical world with an attitude of cooperation and reverence. It is this truth that is so evidently present in Dennis's new book, *Your (Re)Defining Moments*."

—*Rev. Dr. Kenn Gordon, spiritual leader for Centers for Spiritual Living*

"*Your (Re)Defining Moments* by Dennis Merritt Jones is a must-read for everyone on the spiritual path. He is a true Spiritual Master who graciously shares his wisdom, allowing it to unfold in your own mind as gently as a rose opens to bloom. Dr. Jones has written a modern, twenty-first-century guidebook for seekers of truth and students of spirituality. I predict this book will be used as curricula by many teachers."

—*Chris Michaels, author of* The Power of You

"*Your (Re)Defining Moments* is a powerful antidote to aimless and hollow living. Dennis Merritt Jones has crystallized a path of awakening to free us from the trance states of limiting personal assumptions and inauthentic purposes. Reading this wonderful book is like a deep caress . . . a precious homecoming with the miracle and magic seeded in each of our souls."

—*Dr. Roger W. Teel, spiritual leader at Mile Hi Church, Denver, Colorado*

"*Your (Re)Defining Moments* offers a most compelling and convincing opportunity for us all to remember who we have come here to be. In this book, Dennis Merritt Jones brings a gift of extraordinary insightfulness to everyone who seeks spiritual awakening."

—*Rev. Dr. John B. Waterhouse, president of Centers for Spiritual Living*

"Through personal anecdotes and probing questions to the reader, *Your (Re)Defining Moments* gives us access to an engaging self-study on the nature of being and how to live a thoughtful and authentic life. Dennis Merritt Jones's down-to-earth style and direct approach to spirituality makes reading this book enjoyable and soul-satisfying. Balanced with sincere kindness and a gentle sense of humor, this book takes on big ideas such as redefining original sin, reexamining the pursuit of happiness, and admitting we have to let go of some of the past, to make room for what can be. Dennis's latest book confirms why I have been a longtime fan of his writing: it's inspiring, thought provoking, and encouraging."

—*Edward Viljoen, author of* The Power of Meditation

"In *Your (Re)Defining Moments*, Dennis Merritt Jones wisely guides his readers into a joyful exploration and discovery of their Original Self, which was shot out of eternity into this three-dimensional world to deliver their gifts, talents, and skills as only they can."

—*Michael Bernard Beckwith, author of* Life Visioning: A Transformative Process for Activating Your Unique Gifts and Highest Potential

"Here is a book for those who have read the books, done the workshops, but still sense their own epiphanies are simpler, deeper, closer. If personal identity as we have come to know it is a socially constructed wilderness, Dr. D. paves a direct path through the classic conundrums of consciousness—the sovereign Self of Western civilization, the transcendent No-Self of mysticism and the East, and the pristine Now Moment that thrives only in our choice to honor its worth."

—Dr. Barbara E. Fields, executive director of the Association for Global New Thought, director of Gandhi King Season for Nonviolence, director of The Synthesis Dialogues with His Holiness the Dalai Lama, and former program director of Parliament of the World's Religions

"You could spend a lifetime searching for your authentic Self, and defining who you are. Or you could read Dennis Merritt Jones's beautiful new book, Your (Re)Defining Moments, and be gently fast-tracked through the process. Life begins with each moment, with each choice. This is an easy one."

—Lissa Coffey, celebrity lifestyle and wellness expert and author of What's Your Dharma?: Discover the Vedic Way to Your Life's Purpose

"Your (Re)Defining Moments . . . is an amazing book! Dennis Merritt Jones is masterful, guiding us to a deep state of soul remembrance. He reminds us that we were born to be fully expressed and that each moment is an opportunity to choose greatness."

—Cynthia James, author and speaker

"Dennis Merritt Jones's newest work, Your (Re)Defining Moments, makes the powerful distinction between personal discovery and personal 'uncovery.' Ours is not a journey forward but a vertical plunge inward to what has always existed. Liberating and gloriously written, Your (Re)Defining Moments is a treasured contribution to a welcomed renaissance in spiritual literature."

—Dr. David Ault, author of Where Regret Cannot Find Me

"In Your (Re)Defining Moments, Dennis Merritt Jones offers a compass that leads us inward to the authentic Self, that unique spark of Life we were the moment we were born. Dennis reminds us that we still are that unique being and proves it by giving us clear, practical, loving guidance on how to courageously bring our authentic Self to daily life. When you read this book you will embark on the journey of becoming who you were born to be."

—Dr. Cherie Carter-Scott, MCC, author of the New York Times bestseller If Life Is a Game, These Are the Rules

"Dennis Merritt Jones's writing reminds me of a cashmere blanket—warm and comfortable without being too heavy. This book encourages the reader to rework their lives without being preachy or overly challenging. A perfect read before bed."

—Rev. Kathianne Lewis, DD, senior minister and spiritual leader, Centers for Spiritual Living

Your
(Re)Defining
Moments

Your (Re)Defining Moments

Becoming
Who You Were
Born to Be

❋

Dennis Merritt Jones

Jeremy P. Tarcher/Penguin
a member of Penguin Group (USA)
New York

JEREMY P. TARCHER/PENGUIN
Published by the Penguin Group
Penguin Group (USA) LLC
375 Hudson Street
New York, New York 10014

USA · Canada · UK · Ireland · Australia
New Zealand · India · South Africa · China

penguin.com
A Penguin Random House Company

Minimal portions of this book originally appeared in different form in the following
publications: *The Huffington Post* and *The Acorn Newspaper.*

Most Tarcher/Penguin books are available at special quantity discounts for bulk
purchase for sales promotions, premiums, fund-raising, and educational needs.
Special books or book excerpts also can be created to fit specific needs.
For details, write: Special.Markets@us.penguingroup.com.

Library of Congress Cataloging-in-Publication Data

Jones, Dennis Merritt.
Your redefining moments : becoming who you were born to be / Dennis Merritt Jones.
p.   cm.
ISBN 978-0-399-16580-1
1. Self-realization.   2. Self.   3. Introspection.   I. Title.
BJ1470.J59   2014   2013050985
299'.93—dc23

Printed in the United States of America
1   3   5   7   9   10   8   6   4   2

Book design by Katy Riegel

It is with great love and respect that I dedicate this book to my daughter, Merritt Renee Jones, one of the most authentic, joyful, courageous, compassionate, and kind human beings on this planet. The moment she was born, my life was redefined in ways words fail to articulate. Why her soul chose me to be her father my mind cannot comprehend, but my heart shall forever be grateful.

———

Contents

Your
(Re)Defining
Moments

INTRODUCTION

The Question
We'll Have to Face

When you die and go to heaven, our maker is not going to
ask, Why didn't you discover the cure for such and such? The
only question we will be asked in that precious moment is,
Why didn't you become you?

—ELIE WIESEL

I often wonder how many of us are living our lives based on
who we are *not* rather than who we truly are. Since the day
we were born, we learned to define ourselves primarily based on
the input of others. Over the years, that information, be it correct or incorrect, embedded itself deeply in our personal belief
system, far beyond our conscious knowing that it even exists. If
we were to excavate the deepest recesses of our consciousness,
we would discover many beliefs about ourselves that are simply
not true and that may never have been true. Yet we live from
these beliefs as if they were true because we have never identified them clearly enough to question them, to challenge them.

We may have defined ourselves in a limiting way based on
our history and the opinion of others, or after we've suffered a
job loss, failed out of school, gone through a devastating divorce,

experienced a painful health crisis, reduced our material status, were abused, lost a loved one, and so on . . . and we stay stuck there, wearing labels attached to those people and events because we fail to recognize there is a door right in front of us providing another opportunity to (re)define who we are *today*. This is the power to be found in our (re)defining moments; they create an opening for us to *consciously* challenge old ideas and beliefs about who we think we are by accessing the limitless new possibilities that lie inherent in the authentic self. But what is this "self"—where exactly is it, and what makes it "authentic"? These are questions we were born to explore, understand, and apply the answer to in our daily lives. You may consider this a guidebook to help you fathom the depths of your own understanding of your authentic self and, equally important, your being—the Original Self from which you have come.

> "As you go deeper into yourself, you will naturally come to realize that there is an aspect of your being that is always there and never changes . . . This is the root Self. You are not your thoughts; you are aware of your thoughts. You are not your emotions; you feel your emotions. You are not your body; you look at it in the mirror and experience this world through its eyes and ears. You are the conscious being who is aware that you are aware of these inner and outer things."
> —MICHAEL A. SINGER, *The Untethered Soul*

As a dedicated student of ontology—the study of the nature of existence, or being—I believe there is no more compelling quest upon which to embark than the pilgrimage back to our point of origin, for it is there that we may begin to remember a vital part of ourselves we had long forgotten; that mystical place where the

Original "root" Self lives—that aspect of our being that has always been, is now, and shall always be there. Before we set foot on the journey, the question to be derived from the above quote from Michael Singer's inspiring book, *The Untethered Soul*, is, if you are not your thoughts, emotions, or body, who are you—really—and where does that part of "you" live? The tendency is to think about this nebulous Self as existing at the center of our body, somewhere in the vicinity of our chest cavity, but that is a construct our rational, thinking mind came up with because it likes to deal in certainties.

Because of the way our logical mind processes abstract ideas, throughout this book I refer to the "center of your being" as a point within where what you will come to know as your authentic self is to be found. In this context, the word *being* may be considered a noun, not a verb, as it is another term for that part of you that is cognizant of its oneness with the Self. In broader terms, I invite you to think of the center of your being as a place within your consciousness that extends far beyond the confines of your body. This is because the "being" you are spills well over the boundaries of your physical body. The miracle and the mystery of this quest is to arrive at a point where you are "aware that you are aware" that, as Walt Whitman put it, you are not all contained between your hat and your boots. Herein lies the bridge we shall cross: is it enough to declare that the real "you" is this etheric Self? Is it possible that "that" which we refer to as our "authentic self" is simply our "being," an individuated aspect of the Original Self, which is the infinite Intelligence behind all creation, by means of which we each access and express our own unique individuality and purpose? The real question is, how does this knowledge serve you in your daily life? To sincerely ask these questions and follow where they lead serves as our true North Star; it's the journey of finding our way back to our original point of being and *actualizing* that being in our daily lives. In other words, it is a process of consciously becoming that which, in truth, we already are—and thus the subtitle of this book: *Becoming Who You Were Born to Be*. The operative word here is *becoming*. Philosophically and ontologically speaking, "becoming" is the *dynamic* aspect of being. It is taking the noun "being" and turning it into a verb. Simply put, becoming who you were born to be is an ongoing process of consciously bringing the true being you have *always* been into your daily doing. As you'll soon see, it really is the journey of a lifetime.

THE IMPORTANCE
OF YOUR (RE)DEFINING MOMENTS

"We are constantly invited to be who we are."
—HENRY DAVID THOREAU

(Re)defining moments offer us the opportunity to perpetually reinvent ourselves, and as long as we occupy a human body, these opportunities will continue to present themselves. You were born to be you, to unfold the truth of who you are. The same is true for everyone else. Every moment has the potential to be a (re)defining moment when we utilize the opportunity to look more deeply into the mystery of the true Self and learn how to actualize Its qualities in our daily lives. The goal is to increase our awareness that, irrespective of where we are or what we are doing, there stands before us a door in every present moment that, when consciously opened, invites us to step into a deeper knowing of who we truly are. In other words, every encounter (chance or otherwise), event, or circumstance, be it good or bad, right or wrong, happy or sad, is a portal to a (re)defining moment and who we will choose to be in that situation. The question to consider is, will we be consciously present enough in the moment to recognize the opening when it occurs and step through the door, or will our mind be too full of distractions?

KNOWING WHAT TO LET GO OF IS CRUCIAL TO YOUR PILGRIMAGE

A prerequisite to stepping through those portals leading to our (re)defining moments means we might have to let go of some of what "has been" required to make room for what "can be." As you'll soon discover, I love the use of metaphor and stories when attempting to make a salient point. There is no better example of the necessity of letting go of that which may hold us back from living an authentic life and the (re)defining moments that make it possible than the Camino de Santiago. Also referred to as the "Pilgrim's Way," the Camino de Santiago is an ancient trail, dating to the Middle Ages, that runs among a number of countries in Europe and Santiago, Spain. For more than eight centuries, people from all over the world have traversed the trail. At its farthest point, the trail is about 500 miles long, going from St. Jean-Pied-du-Port near Biarritz, France, to Santiago, Spain. In ancient times, besides being a trade route, the trail served as a route that pilgrims from all over Europe walked to reach Santiago for religious reasons, including receiving absolution at the shrine of St. James. Today, thousands of "pilgrims" walk the trail every year, but for many, with a different goal in mind—it is not just about reaching Santiago, it is about the experience gained along the way. It is said that many of those who walk the trail today do so as a ritual to find a part of themselves they feel they have lost touch with or, in many cases, never knew existed. If this sounds like the pilgrimage we are about to take together in this book, that's because it is.

For the dedicated traveler, it can take better than a month to walk the trail. A friend and colleague of mine, Dr. David Ault, who walked the Camino de Santiago several years ago, told me that completing the journey caused him to "die many deaths." This was his way of saying he had to let go of lots of "stuff" he was very attached to, both materially and emotionally, along the trail. He said that "one discovers how necessary it is to let loose of physical baggage in order to make the more than 500-mile journey possible." Along the way, David says, "Receptacle bins line the path through the famous Pyrenees as pilgrims unload unnecessary items, realizing they have brought entirely too much weight for the journey."

The metaphor of David's journey is rich with meaning: while we may not be physically burdened with heavy backpacks on our pilgrimage through the pages of this book, many of us carry emotional baggage crammed full of "stuff" that may impede our progress. Many of us are weighed down with old, repetitive, and less-than-productive thoughts and memories. Some of us will begin the journey with preconceived ideas and outdated beliefs that may not fit through the portal of a (re)defining moment, so we might need to place them in a receptacle bin along the way. When we are willing to set aside the contents of an "overstuffed" mind and walk the trail unburdened, we'll discover that it's difficult *not* to hear what the heart wants to say. If we are willing to listen, we'll be guided to many (re)defining moments, leading us to an authentic life, a life filled with purpose, meaning, and perhaps most important, a deep and abiding sense of peace that only comes to us when we are being who we know we came here to be. This is the journey back to the place we really never left; this is the quest we set upon in this book—to free ourselves to be who we truly are. If are you a seeker and you are ready to embark on the journey, the portal to your next (re)defining moment lies just ahead. Are you ready to see where it takes you?

How to Use This Book to Your Greatest Advantage

If you have read any of my other writings, you already know I am a strong advocate of conscious self-inquiry. As with my other books, here, too, you will discover "Points to Ponder and Personalize" at the end of each chapter. Each Point to Ponder offers you an opportunity to consider how you can realize, personalize, and apply the ideas presented in each chapter in your daily life. As one of my teachers once put it, "Realization, without application, is hallucination."

Scattered at different points throughout the book, you'll also find mindfulness practices designed to assist you in identifying, challenging, and transcending the hidden beliefs that have defined you until now. The intended result is an increased awareness of the (re)defining moments that lead you back to the true you, where creating an authentic life truly worth living occurs.

A Note to the Reader about the Use of Capitalized Words

In this book, I occasionally use terms that I have capitalized, such as the *Self*, the *Original Self*, and the *true Self* to highlight their importance to the discussion at hand. The term *Self*, and its several variations, is synonymous with the initiating, omnipresent, universal, infinite intelligence behind all creation. These words are not meant to be confused with the human "self," meaning that part of us that is conscious and able to think and talk about ourselves as both a subject and an object. Lastly, I use terms such as *Life*, the *One*, the *Beloved*, *Presence*, *Light*, and *Being* interchangeably with the *Self*, based on the context in which they are being used because they essentially mean the same thing to me. I realize that some are very comfortable with the term *Self* in a spiritual vein and others will relate to the word only in a more secular context. In either case, I am more focused on the idea that, irrespective of whatever wording you resonate with at your core, you embrace the idea that there is more for you to know about who you are and can be.

What do you have to gain by living an authentic life? The answer is profoundly simple: a sense of inner peace, purpose, and freedom that affects every area of your life, from your relationships to your work, to your physical, emotional, and spiritual well-being. This is the quest we set upon in this book—to recognize our (re)defining moments and use them as the springboard to living an authentic life, freeing ourselves to express who we truly are. This is the journey of becoming who we were born to be.

I am pleased and honored to have you as my traveling companion on this journey. It promises to be a life-changing pilgrimage. Let the adventure begin!

Peace,
Dennis

CHAPTER 1

Being an Original Begins Here

The (Re)Defining Moment You Were Born to Have

Our lives are a series of defining moments, strung together by passing time. Surrender fully to this moment, because it is not the moment itself that defines us, but how we choose to live in it.

—JILL PENDLEY

On a trip to Rome, my wife and I had the good fortune of being hosted for a private tour of the Vatican. It was a sticky, hot, autumn day with wall-to-wall people from every corner of the globe moving slowly through the monolithic complex. As we walked the historic halls and galleries, some dating back 1,600 years, our guide, Stephan, paused and said, "This is a very typical day here in Vatican City . . . there will be about 25,000 people who will pass through these corridors today, each on a pilgrimage of their own making. Many people come to see the historical sights, and some come to seek a deeper part of themselves—to reconnect with their ancient roots—to be reminded that they are part of something much larger than themselves that they seldom think about."

Stephan's comments also tell us of our story. There are those of us who shuffle through life as if it were a museum where our entire lives are on display—day by day adding another bit of history that influences and shapes our beliefs in ways that we may not pause to fully comprehend. At the beginning of our personal metaphoric tour, there is a moment when we are each born, and at the end of the tour, a moment when we each die; the space in between those two events is a continuum of moments, which, when strung together, we call our life. Between the coming and the going, we walk through the halls of our daily lives, spending countless unconscious moments staring at our own personal history. As we pass each display (event or experience), we seldom stop to contemplate that each experience is adding to our minds another layer of belief about ourselves and life that, ultimately, defines who we think we are. Many of us believe that we are no more than the sum of our experiences, and we have a plethora of evidence to prove this is so—we talk about it, we take plenty of pictures and video, and we share our history with others who are on a similar tour of the museum. While this is not necessarily a bad thing, I refer to living at this level of life as existing horizontally, "living on the surface." When we live on the surface of life, we believe that life is something that happens *to* us rather than *through* us, and we are unknowingly inviting the ever-changing conditions that occur on the surface of everyday life to shape us. That is a powerless and potentially unfulfilling place in which to exist.

And then one day, when it is our time to leave the museum, with our final breath, we may realize that, perhaps, just maybe, there could have been more to our lives; a deeper exploration and dimension of living than what we experienced . . . but we missed it by moving through each day as if we were being herded through an ever-crowded parade of passing events. My point is that by living on the surface of life, many of us squander our entire existence, spending countless precious moments being defined by our surface experiences, living from the outside in rather than the inside out. Living on the surface is probably easier and more comfortable, but we will never find the truth of who we really are by skimming the surface of life.

What Awaits Us Below Surface Living?

"Direct your eye inward, and you'll find
A thousand regions in your mind
Yet undiscovered. Travel them and be
Expert in home-cosmography."
—HENRY DAVID THOREAU, *Walden*

For many of us (until now), life has been more about getting by, surviving, and staying safe—essentially enduring life until we exit the planet. Why is it that so many of us seem to live lives that are less than deeply rewarding, enjoyable, and fully expressed? Because we exist in a horizontal world where living vertically is not the norm. We have wandered astray; we have forgotten we are a child of the infinite Universe and lost our way, spending increasingly more time living horizontally on the surface, each day moving farther and farther, it seems, from the authentic self we knew ourselves to be at birth.

To illustrate this point, just go to a park or playground and watch young children "being" themselves at play. Listen to their words and observe their behavior, and you'll see and hear real authenticity. That is because they are still navigating life in a vertical manner; they are not yet trapped on the surface of life. Then go to a nightclub or any work environment, and watch and listen to adults "doing" whatever they do. You will see and hear something quite different as they perform roles that they have acquired through various cultural mandates. The problem is, too often, they forget it's only a role they are playing; they have become so absorbed in their roles, they forget who they "truly" are.

On the other hand, in a natural and safe environment, young children do not perform for others, even when playing with one another. They express themselves freely and authentically . . . until they grow older and learn to do otherwise to survive, or so they think—and the role-playing begins. The more years we have lived, the more we have forgotten from where we've come and *why* we have come to this life. Many of us have become so disconnected from our authentic self, it's as if we are wandering through life with no compass—no sense of who we are, or where we are going, or what we are doing here in the first place. Our soul knows who we truly are and what we are doing here. The good news is, if we are willing to access and follow our internal guidance system (the intuition continually being emitted from the soul), it is preprogrammed to seek our center, to guide us vertically, back to the authentic self.

Yes . . . You Are *That* Important

"There is a vitality, a life force, an energy, a quickening that is translated through you into action, and because there is only one of you in all time, this expression is unique. And if

you block it, it will never exist through any other medium
and will be lost."

—MARTHA GRAHAM

Inherent in every living thing is an insatiable hunger, the innate
desire to express life by freely and fully being "what" it was
uniquely created to be. To personalize this, consider the possibility that there was a time when you were a "what" before you
were a "who." If you can wrap your mind around that possibility, then, the question to explore is, *what* were you before you
became a *who*—and why did you become the *who* you uniquely
are when there are so many other "who"s on the planet you
might have been? While this may seem like a bit of a paradoxical tongue twister, it is the quintessential question that requires
exploration if you are to follow *your* true North Star back to
your point of origin, where you'll find your authentic self waiting to weave itself into the fabric of your human life *today* and
every day.

Make no mistake about it, this is the sojourn you were born
to make, not just once but many times in your life, each time
returning, from your center, to the surface of your life with a
deeper awareness of who you truly are beneath the trappings of
the egoic-self and a world that defines itself by what lies of the
surface. The "practice" (a term I use throughout this book that
invites you to consider taking a specific action regarding the
topic at hand) is to learn how to consciously bring your authentic "being" into your human "doing," which is where vertical
living and horizontal living intersect. Your (re)defining moments will open the portals to vertical living along the way that
get you there. In the process of reconnecting with your authen-

tic self, you may be led to fully understand the significance of your life and how important *you,* as an individual, really are, to the whole of life. Now let's take a look at why this is so.

In the Beginning, There Was Only Life, and There Still Is Only Life

"The great mystics have been illumined. They have seen through the veil of matter and perceived the Spiritual Universe . . . All emerge from that One Whose Being is ever present and Whose Life, robed in numberless forms, is manifest throughout all Creation. Creation is the logical result of the outpush of Life into self-expression."

—ERNEST HOLMES

About fourteen billion years ago (give or take a few billion) the first chapter of the greatest miracle and mystery of all time began when something beyond all human logic and comprehension happened—the Ethers of that which, for countless millennia, would become known to humankind by many different names, including the Original Self, began to stir. This was the initiating sacred spark of Life; in a flash, self-igniting, giving birth to, and manifesting the idea of Itself. In the process of unfolding, from within and by means of its own creative nature, it left, and continues to leave, in its wake, stars, planets, and galaxies far beyond our ability to count. It is common knowledge that stars group together in formations called galaxies. The Sun under which we bask on summer days is just another slightly above-average-size star known as a yellow dwarf and belongs to the Milky Way galaxy. Astronomers tell us there are about 100 thousand million stars in the Milky Way alone. Even more astounding, the Universe consists of millions upon millions of galaxies . . . and is still expanding at the speed of light (and some scientists are now saying even faster than the speed of light) without showing any sign of slowing down. I don't even pretend to understand the physics of how this all happened or continues to happen, but I invite you to just sit for a moment with that information and breathe. To contemplate the vastness and the expansiveness of this living organism called "Universe" can be rather mind-boggling, especially when you consider that *you* are part of it.

> "The Universe is an infinite sphere, the center of
> which is everywhere, the circumference nowhere."
> —BLAISE PASCAL

It is clear we exist in an abundant living Universe that knows no restriction—only the impulse to eternally expand with no limits or boundaries, perpetually becoming more of what it is and can ever be—star-stuff . . . Life, pushing out by creating light and matter from *within* itself, shaping and giving form *to* itself, exquisitely clothing itself in an infinite and unique number of ways. To even entertain the notion we exist in a living Universe is to open ourselves to the fact that there is an Intelligence at work in our lives; beyond that surpasses our ability to fully comprehend. The only thing we need do is look to the midnight sky and witness the order and pattern of the stars and planets and how they are held in place. Better still, take just a few minutes to sit and gaze into the petals of a rose and think about how it unfolds. Or look into a newborn baby's eyes and witness firsthand "star-stuff" forming in ever-new, unique, and beautiful ways. This is the mystery and miracle of Life at work and Infinite Intelligence creating more of itself out of itself. Does that not evoke a sense of awe and reverence for the gift called life?

Living Vertically in a Horizontal World

This is a guidebook for seekers, those unique individuals who are on a conscious quest to experience a more authentic approach to everyday life, those who want to live closer to that essence of the pure beings they were when they were born and which they know will never be found on the surface of a horizontally lived life. This book is written for those who are on a pilgrimage of their own making, those who are compelled to live vertically and go deeper, to the true core of their being, to explore the hidden caverns of a life they have never consciously known before. Within the heart of the true seeker lies an inherent wisdom that silently whispers, "Before you can live an authentic life, you must first know who it is you authentically are." Those seeking to live a more authentic life inherently know it requires great courage to go deeper—beyond their known "history" and where, for the first time, they intentionally connect with their roots and affirm they are part of something much larger than they have ever experienced while living superficially on the surface of life. Why does this journey take courage? Because it requires a willingness to be forever changed—literally transformed—by, not only what, but *who* they find on this inward sojourn.

> "At the center of your being you have the answer; you know who you are and you know what you want."
>
> —LAO TZU

Whether we are consciously aware of it or not, we are each in our own way seeking something that anchors us in life; we seek something to believe in—something that gives our life a sense of solidity, relevance, purpose, and meaning. Connecting to something larger than ourselves is an ancient quest, one seekers have embarked upon for millennia. It seems to be a call we all hear and yet it is a pilgrimage relatively few choose to ever undertake. This is truly a journey of one's own making because it can only be taken by the individual—one step at a time—and more specifically, one *moment* at a time. The profound reward in taking the journey is that any single "one" of those moments can be *the* moment that (re)defines your entire life. In those moments, you get a glimpse of the ancient roots that connect you to that "something" with which you intrinsically sense you are eternally connected. Once you experience what that is, you'll never be the same because it will draw you to a deeper understanding of the unique, one-of-a-kind being you really are and were born to be. In short, in that moment, your life will be (re)defined. As Lao Tzu said, at your center you already know who you are and what you want. Now it's time to dive in and bring who you truly are to the surface and claim the authentic life that is yours to live.

A Defining Moment Doesn't Add Anything *to* You, It Reveals Something *in* You

Some of us might think of a defining moment as something that happens on the battlefield or in a crisis where, in the heat of the moment, we exhibit an aspect of our true character that defines us in the eyes of others as a hero. But those are not the only kind available. There are also those defining moments that are far more personal, ones that cannot be perceived by others; those moments that, in a singular instant, are so profoundly impactful, they forever alter how we see ourselves and, thus, how we interface with life.

Many of us would be able to pinpoint a specific event or time in our lives when something happened that gave us pause to not only remember that singular moment but also look deeply enough *into* it to see a part of ourselves that, until that moment, we had no idea was there . . . and to be changed forever by what we experienced. These moments are the portal to where living an authentic life begins.

The Great Paradox of a True (Re)defining Moment

Regardless of how we may each interpret what a "defining moment" is, the practice is to remember that we are not restricted to having only one of them in our lifetime. Any moment can be a (re)defining moment because within it lies the opportunity to be changed by what we see and experience, that which can indelibly etch an imprint of who we see ourselves to be on our mind and heart that shapes the life before us. In those moments, we have the opportunity to, metaphorically, drill into the deepest core of our being and bear witness to what lies within, remembering that those moments will not add something to us, but rather reveal something *within* us. It's not about discovering anything; it's a moment of unearthing that which is *already* there and has always been there—the Original Self, which, as we'll discover, is only one of many names for the originating Intelligence behind all of life. Some might as easily refer to the Original Self as Universe, Presence, God, the Self, Brahman, Atman, Source, Life, Infinite One, I AM, Being, the Whole, Divine Mind, the Beloved, Allah, the Great Spirit, Creator, and even It.

The Original Self lives in each of us, but only to the degree that we first understand we live in It. This paradox is one that has perplexed humankind from antiquity. In his book, *The Living Universe,* visionary Duane Elgin writes, "In exploring our cosmic identity, it is important to recognize our paradoxical nature: we are each unique, yet totally connected to the entire universe. We are each original and there will never be another person like us in all eternity. At the same time, since our existence arises from and is woven into the deep ecology of the universe, we are completely integrated with all that exists. Both unity and uniqueness are integral to our nature." In other words, what we might refer to as our authentic self is simply that unique and *individuated* point within us that is *unlike* any other human being on the planet, where the Original Self has personalized Itself. The practice is to become skillful at bringing that uniqueness into our horizontal lives by bringing our true "being" into our daily "doing." The access point that integrates the two can only be found in the present moment. This, in itself, means that every moment of our lives holds the potential to be a (re)defining moment.

Recognizing Your Unique Place in the Big Picture Can Be a (Re)Defining Moment

"The lamps are different,
But the Light is the same.

One matter, one energy, one Light, one Light-mind,
Endlessly emanating all things."

—RUMI

I remember, as a kid, laying on the grass at night staring at the stars in wide-eyed wonderment, contemplating where the edge of the Universe was and what the heck I was doing there in the middle of it. While I didn't fully comprehend it at the time as the Original Self, I inherently knew I was one with something far greater than myself, and that awareness alone gave me a sense of inner peace I carry with me to this day. Perhaps you can relate: understanding the immensity of a Universe expanding at the speed of light, your perspective of it is crucial; it will either make you feel small, insignificant, separate, and apart "from" it all or, conversely, a large and significant part "of" it all. In the words of astronomer Carl Sagan, "The cosmos is within us. We are made of star-stuff. We are a way for the universe to know itself." My point is, you *are* part of it all, regardless of whether you know it, or like it, or not. However, in establishing your awareness of your oneness with the Universe—the Original Self—you'll be more likely to find your place *in* it as you begin to experience (re)defining moments that put you on the vertical path, leading you back to your authentic self.

"The authentic self is soul made visible."
—SARAH BAN BREATHNACH

Beyond the mystery of *how* the Universe gave birth to itself, the deeper question lies in pondering *why* it gave birth to itself, and to you. Why are you here? With all the grandeur and the sheer magnitude of the Universe, why are *you*—*specifically you*—here? Your soul's invisible presence in the world is embedded in you as your authentic self. Its role is to be the emissary of the Original Self from which it came; its purpose is to circumnavigate the totality of your life, exploring the terrain of the human condition and gathering information for its own evolution through direct contact and experience with the world of people, places, and things on the surface of life. From the depths of its innate connection to the whole, the soul integrates itself with your body, which Duane Elgin refers to as a "biodegradable vehicle." Think about that! Your body, for all intents and purposes, is a disposable, carbon-based vessel the soul commissioned and boarded for the journey and will, likewise, jettison at the completion of the journey, returning it to the stardust elements from which it, too, came. When we remember this, we'll be able to see that the commingling of our soul and our body is where and when the *what* and the *who*, which have always been one, fully merge in our conscious awareness.

Bringing Together the What and the Who

The practice is to learn how to mindfully bring as much of *what* you are into the expression of *who* you are in the present moment. Again, this is accomplished as the authentic self vertically merges with your daily horizontal life. With a little bit of conscious intention, this happens organically as the essence of the intangible "Original Self" subtly rises and commingles with the tangible "self" and ties the knot, unifying the two as one. In this process, the imagined line between the *what* and the *who* dissolves. I say the line is imagined because it never really existed; we invented it when we entered this life plain and started forgetting who we really were. It is important to remember that while the Universe is greater than the sum of its parts, the Universe is wholly contained within and *as* each of its parts, meaning you and me. Perhaps Ernest Holmes stated it more eloquently when he wrote, "The One encompasses and flows through All, spilling Itself into numberless forms, and personalities." That is quite a visualization, isn't it? Can you imagine the Original Self "spilling" Itself into a template called "you," manifesting as spirit, mind, and body? In addition, consider the fact that the template called "you" could be used only *once* for all eternity—that is how unique you are *and* how important you are to the congruency and wholeness of an expanding Universe.

Your Pilgrimage Begins Now

The pilgrimage of this book is one of remembrance: throughout are numerous guideposts and mindfulness practices specifically designed and strategically placed along the way to gently remind us of our ancient roots.

Living closer to the center of our being is the practice of a lifetime. While it is the road less traveled, there is a pathway for seekers that guides us there, a pathway lined with one defining moment after another if we learn how to mindfully connect to them in our daily life. What if we were to reconfigure our concept of "a" defining moment and elongate it? What if we could be so mindful on our pilgrimage that our life becomes a sacred continuum, a series of (re)defining moments in which we connect the dots, each one seamlessly linked, taking us deeper, below surface living, allowing us to see more clearly who we were born to be—the authentic self we are and have always been? What if we were to successfully access that authentic part of us that finds its ancient roots in that "something larger than ourselves" and mindfully bring it to the surface, into our lives today and every day? Can you imagine yourself living your life from the inside out, so courageously, so transparently, so authentically that who you really are shows up in every sacred moment? If your answer is "yes," you have just stepped into your next (re)defining moment.

While (re)defining moments are more fully discussed in subsequent chapters, as you set your intention to consciously evolve through living vertically, (re)defining moments appear as they are needed. *They are drawn to you* sequentially to support you in the process of your own evolution, each one a perfectly aligned portal in space and time, opening and closing, creating whatever experience is required to guide you back to the authentic self where you began this amazing journey. The question is, will you see the portals when they open and, more important, will you step through them before they close?

POINTS TO PONDER AND PERSONALIZE

• Does the term "Original Self" resonate with you? Knowing there are many names for the originating Intelligence behind all life, if another term is more relatable to you, feel free to use it. Any word you use is but a symbol that is yours to relate with in whatever manner makes it personal to you. The Original Self doesn't care what you call it, as long as you call it forward to live authentically in your daily life.

- Do you recognize the wisdom found in the sentiment by Lao Tzu that before you can live an authentic life, you must first know who it is you authentically are? As he says, at your center, you *already* know who you are. When you are connected to that center, any moment can be a (re)defining moment.

- Are you currently living your life more on the horizontal path or the vertical path? To paraphrase the words of my Vatican guide, Stephan, some of us see our lives from a historical (horizontal) perspective, while others seek a deeper part of themselves (vertical), to reconnect with their ancient roots, to be reminded that they are part of something much larger than themselves. Which is your journey? The key is to incorporate a daily practice that allows you to mindfully enter the vertical path with an openness to see where it will take you. Reading this book is a clear statement of your intention because the seeker within you already is packed and ready for the journey . . . this book simply points the way.

- How does it feel to think of your body as "star-stuff" that is the soul's home on the journey called your life? You can start to process this profound idea by remembering that *who* you are (a conscious, thinking, human being with a name and a body) determines how much of *what* you are (your authentic self) makes it to the surface of life to be expressed.

As a Mindfulness Practice,
Consider the Following:

Carry a journal with you for the next few days. At different times throughout the day, stop and take note of where your mind is in that moment. Are you more focused on living horizontally (your outer world) or vertically (your inner world)? Remember, balance is the key. The practice is not to linger at your center *or* on the surface of life, but mindfully, moment by moment, transition between the two, bringing your authentic being into your human doing. When doing this simple mindfulness practice, don't be surprised if you see a (re)defining moment opening right before your eyes. Yes, it really is that easy. Now breathe and dive in!

Chapter 2

You Are Hardwired to Express

You Can Run, but You Can't Hide from
the Urge to Be Who You Were Born to Be

There is an urge to express in all people, and this urge, operating through the channels of the Creative Mind, looses energy into action, and compels the individual to do something.

—Ernest Holmes

I will never forget the first time I opened a bottle of "sparkling" wine—it was in my younger days while at a wedding reception for one of my college buddies. Being a less-than-sophisticated drinker, I didn't really understand what "sparkling" meant until I nearly put the bride's eye out with a cork flying just under mach 1 as it exited the bottle. Other than a lump on her forehead, she survived just fine. Suffice it to say, that was followed by an eruption of foam and bubbles that created quite a mess . . . and, thankfully, some laughter as well. Needless to say, I quickly discovered that one isn't supposed to jostle a bottle of sparkling wine and then remove the cork too quickly. Over the past four and a half decades, and after opening a fair number of bottles without endangering anyone else's life, I have learned one needs to remove the cork very, *very* mindfully, controlling the release of excess carbonation, allowing it to slowly escape. The reason this works is because you are *intentionally* directing the flow of the compressed energy (in this case, in the form of carbonation) seeking release from the container in which it has been "trapped." Once you have mastered this technique, you are, metaphorically speaking, an "energy director."

What does all this have to do with your (re)defining moments and finding your way back to the authentic self? The same dynamic principle applies when directing the energy of the unexpressed Self that has been bottled up at your core, sometimes for a long time: once conscious of Its presence and need for expression, you can direct how that energy flows. As a verb, the word *express* means "to push out," which is exactly what the energy behind the innate urge of the authentic self does—it pushes out, it seeks a creative outlet through you, and eventually it *will* have its way. In the long run, if you create an intentional opening through which this energy may express in a healthy manner, it will do so. If you fail to direct this innate desire mindfully, however, it will still have its way, and you may not care for the consequences.

In other words, energy will find a way out from your center to the surface of your life. It will create *something*—it *must* create something—but you determine what it will create. Once you are aware that within you lies a condensed energy propelling the desire to authentically express yourself—to be who you truly are—you can direct it mindfully in a manner that serves you extremely well as you approach your (re)defining moments. (Re)defining moments are simply energy vortexes that draw the authentic self up (vertically) and out (horizontally) and into present-moment awareness, revealing it to the light of day and the gifts it holds.

The question is, why would anyone suppress this innate urge to express themselves in an authentic manner? Perhaps they are so out of touch with themselves they can't feel the authentic self stirring. Then again, perhaps they were taught or conditioned *not* to feel it. As we'll discover, that can have some dire consequences.

Coloring Outside the Lines Is Risky Business

It is virtually impossible to have a (re)defining moment without first having established a baseline by means of which we currently define ourselves. That baseline began at our birth and was more than likely established in a litany of fear-based limitations. This is not an indictment of our primary caretakers, be they parents or otherwise. Rather, it is about clearly seeing how much of the life we had not yet lived was defined (and, thus, predetermined) by others who were doing the very best they knew how to do, with only the highest and best for us in mind. Looking back thirty years, I can see myself doing the same thing with my daughter, Merritt, who, thankfully, managed to survive my well-intended, but often misguided, parenting skills.

There can be no doubt that much of a parent's concern for their children lies in the fear of something bad happening to them and, therefore, the information they pass on to their children about being "safe" is appropriate. Many of us probably would not be alive today if we hadn't taken some of our parent's concern for our well-being to heart. Unfortunately, as children, we probably too often interpreted that care and concern to mean life wasn't a safe place—the message, either spoken or implied, was that if we lived within the confines of the boundaries our primary caretak-

ers set, we would be better off, safer. When we ignored that ad-
vice and colored outside the lines, exploring what it meant to be
an individual, we were generally "corrected" and put back in our
place. Each time we were put back in our place, the creative energy seeking a unique pathway of expression through us was
"shaken up," like that uncorked bottle of sparkling wine, becoming more compressed.

Clearly, our caregivers' intentions were good, but what they
didn't realize is that we were only responding to the call of the
authentic self. We were following an inner urge—an ancient,
eternal, internal guidance system we were born with, one pro-
grammed to compel us to follow a path that honors our individuality and inherent need to grow, allowing us to push out
and explore beyond the lines drawn for us by others and *express*
our uniqueness openly and freely. Just watch any toddler in action and you'll see what I mean. They are continually exploring,
wondering, and wandering, with great curiosity, until they are
taught not to. Over a period of enough years, we become quite
efficient at stifling our uniqueness and desire to express it in
acquiescence to the voices of others, regardless of how well in-
tentioned they may or may not have been. The practice is to pay
attention to the call arising from the center of our being.

Hearing the Call and Heeding It Are Two Different Things

"None of us will ever accomplish anything excellent or com-
manding except when he listens to this whisper which is
heard by him alone."

—RALPH WALDO EMERSON

Since that first initiating spark of light emanating as the Original Self, the Universe has impregnated every living thing with a distant call that yearns to be heard. At the moment of your birth, you entered the human condition hardwired to seek freedom—to be an unfettered, one-of-a-kind being. It was at that very moment you heard a quiet whisper in your ear saying, "Here you are, here is your life . . . now go, do, and be who you truly are—be who *you* came here to be." There is a place within you that heard that whisper then, knew it as truth, and still hears it today—and it won't be still until you acknowledge it. In much the same way, the Original Self began to stir before becoming the light and matter of the all that is. A smoldering ember of that original light exists within you today, and it is burning, subtlety stirring the subterranean energy of your soul, trying to get your attention, *re*-calling you, as it were—calling you back from the surface of life to your center—reminding you where you came from, who you truly are, and who you were born to be.

This is self-evident in the fact that you are reading this particular book at this particular time. There are no mistakes. This is an indicator you are starting, once again, to heed the call. I say "once again," because, while you may have been vaguely aware of it for some portion of your life, when you were first born, you had much less clutter and fewer people's voices in your head to distract you. As a young child, therefore, you were in constant contact with the call. You were more intuitive and available to experience your natural urge to push out and explore *beyond* the boundaries others were setting for you. This call is often what got you into hot water with the authority figures in your life when you colored outside the lines . . . in those times when you followed the call off the well-trodden and acceptable path to satisfy your innate curiosity and express yourself authentically.

When you were young, the call was compelling because the memory of the Source of the call was still freshly imprinted in your mind and heart, and you intuitively knew the pathway back to your authentic self. As you grew and became more enmeshed in the beliefs passed down from your parents and other influential authority figures, you were unknowingly being trained to pay less attention to the innate driving force within you that caused you to grow and engage life on your own terms. As Don Miguel Ruiz put it in his classic book, *The Four Agreements*, you became "domesticated," slowly being defined from the outside in by taking on the identity of who others thought you should be—and, in the process, your authentic self got stuffed into a box called conformity where, once tightly sealed inside, it began to, metaphorically, suffocate and eventually fall into a deep sleep resulting in spiritual amnesia.

The Itch That Won't Go Away and the Risk You Take in Scratching It

"And the day came when the risk to remain tight in a bud was more painful than the risk it took to blossom."
—ANAÏS NIN

The challenge, upon awakening, is like a recurring itch that will not go away until it has been thoroughly scratched. For a majority of our lives, most of us have avoided, denied, anesthetized, or otherwise tried to suppress that nudge because, at some level, we feared it could open up the box in which our authentic self was being held captive. Perhaps we sensed that, just like Pandora's box, once opened, we might not be able to close the box again—

and we were right: once we have felt its nudge and heard the ancient, serene song of the authentic self wooing us, we can run but we cannot hide from who we truly are. That is the inherent risk we take when we begin to honor the only self we knew as newborns but began to forget almost immediately.

The Pandora's box to which I am referring is the negativity of a world that wants us to ignore the voice. Why is this so? The world really doesn't want you to remember who you truly are because when you begin to live from the authentic self, the world loses much of its control over you and your behavior. It will do anything in its power to keep you in a dream state wherein the source of your identity is dependent on what's "out there," on the surface of life, rather than what lies within you at your center. (This is where the egoic-self, which will be fully explained in future chapters, begins to take on a life of its own.) If you think I jest about the response of the world to those who seek and promote authentic self-expression, self-reliance, individuality, and the freedom it brings, consider the many individuals throughout history who took such a stand. From Socrates, Jesus, and Gandhi, to Susan B. Anthony, Martin Luther King, Jr., Harvey Milk, and Nelson Mandela, the world has let it be known that to openly and transparently seek the freedom to be who you truly are is risky business. You don't have to be an historical icon to be challenged by the world to stay in your box and stifle your authentic voice. Living from the authentic self is an act of courage for anyone—it's about being willing to lift the lid off the box that has kept you so well hidden, defined, and confined (and safe) for so long and stepping into your true power—especially when it is likely to garner the disapproval of others. Make no mistake about it; stepping out of the box is, in itself, a true (re)defining moment that will change your life forever.

> "We are not supposed to all be the same, feel the same, think the same, and believe the same. The key to continued expansion of our Universe lies in diversity, not in conformity and coercion. Conventionality is the death of creation."
> —ANTHON ST. MAARTEN

To a large degree, the world has been very successful at collectively keeping the lid on the box, but things are changing. More people all around the world are beginning to pay attention to that nudge from within. The quest for freedom of authentic, individual self-expression is becoming the clarion call for hundreds of millions of people everywhere. From civil uprisings in countries all over the world, to the escalated and ongoing various equal rights movements throughout the United States and other regions, the ripple effect of the call coming from the authentic self is being felt universally. A paradigm shift is occurring, and you are part of it. While it may appear different in every culture, individuals are literally rising up and demanding that for which we are all inherently hardwired: the freedom to authentically be who we each have come here to be, to be heard and honored for who we are. Inherent in every living thing lies the desire to be free—*and the power* to make it so. If you consider yourself alive and you can hear the call, you have a standing invitation to join the party—your happiness, well-being, and longevity depend on it.

The Good News and the Other News

"If you bring forth what is within you, what you bring forth
will save you. If you do not bring forth what is within you,
what you do not bring forth will destroy you."
—Gospel of Thomas

Much like a "good news, bad news" punch line, while awakening
to the power and presence of the authentic self is essentially "good
news," some "other news" also comes with it if you are to successfully be open to your (re)defining moments. The good news
is, you have within you a compelling urge to grow and evolve—
to live uniquely, transparently, and freely from that deepest place
of authenticity—where the *who* joyfully commingles with the
what. This, however, is also the "other news": if you don't pay attention to, and honor, this compelling innate urge to express,
grow, and evolve, it will eventually wreak havoc in your life
emotionally and, ultimately, physically. Although it may not appear so on the surface of life, much of what ails our society comes
directly from a suppressed desire to freely be who we truly are.
You cannot push down the innate urge to express your authentic
self without a serious push back from the Universe. The universal
imperative is grow or die; if you fail to pay attention to the innate
desire to push out, that hunger will slowly consume you.

This news should not depress or distress you; it should de-
stress and inspire you. The practice is to remember that energy
will have its way with you and you have no choice in the matter.
However, it is completely yours to determine in *what* manner
that energy will serve you. Just like the condensed carbonated
energy in a bottle of sparkling wine, being mindful of how you

release and direct that energy has everything to do with how much you will enjoy it. The choice is yours and yours alone: a fulfilling life of joyful, authentic self-expression that unfolds with grace and ease . . . or a life filled with angst, regret, and resentment, resulting in a less-than-fulfilling visit on the planet, all because you failed to honor who you truly are. I know which I would choose—how about you?

POINTS TO PONDER AND PERSONALIZE

- Can you relate to my experience with the bottle of sparkling wine and the metaphor behind it? Is any condensed energy of the unexpressed self nudging you? If you just sit with that question and allow yourself to honestly experience what is going on inside you at this moment, you'll know. Just like an itch that won't go away until it is scratched, that nudge, once felt, isn't going anywhere until you do something about it.

- Were you "domesticated" at an early age and taught not to color outside the lines? If so, can you see where it may have spilled over into your adult life? If some residual energy of restriction is still wrapping itself around you, can you feel it beginning to dissipate as you recognize it for what it is? If you have been resisting or denying that nudge, you need not worry. If you take this journey to heart with clear intention, by the time you finish reading this book, you will have danced with, and hopefully transcended, that fear.

- Is there a person, either from the annals of history, or a current-day figure (perhaps someone you know personally) you admire who had the clarity and courage to stand in the truth of their own being, regardless of what the world had to say? If so, consider that person an archetype for you, knowing if he or she could do it, certainly you can as well.

- You are hardwired to seek the freedom to express your authentic self. In much the same way that you can mindfully release and direct the compressed energy trapped in a tightly closed bottle, you also are able to mindfully release and direct the energy of the unexpressed self in a manner that honors who you are and have come here to be—and *that* is the greatest news of all.

CHAPTER 3

Remembering to Remember Who You Really Are

*The Process of Knowing,
and Forgetting, and Remembering Again*

The path of Remembering ultimately requires a decent into
the realms of unknowing . . . The precipice of unknowing is
where Truth is found. Again and again, the paradox!
—RONDA LARUE, *Remembering Who You Really Are*

While riding the bullet train from Rome to Florence, I had a very interesting experience. Let me preface it by saying that traveling at 185 miles per hour on a train that runs incredibly silent and smooth is quite conducive to sleep, especially if you are sleep deprived at the time. After sitting for ten minutes with my gaze fixed on the beautiful Italian countryside, I began to doze off. I thought I was in dreamland when, suddenly and without warning, all sense of peripheral light faded into absolute darkness. Several moments later, while still resting with my eyes closed, bright light instantly filled the cabin for several moments only to, again, go pitch-black. The pattern of the lights snapping on and then off each instant continued for the next half hour. Even with my eyes closed, this was a startling experience because I could still perceive the sudden shifts from light to dark and dark to light. I came to the conclusion that I was having either a flashback to the '60s, the out-of-body experience I always wondered about, or the train was passing through a series of tunnels. Much to my chagrin, it was the latter. All was not lost, however. Always looking for the perfect metaphor, it instantly occurred to me that repeatedly going from light into darkness and darkness into light is akin to the life of one traveling on the railway to enlightenment. The journey back to the authentic self is filled with just such experiences. Finding your way back to who you were born to be is a process of repeatedly passing through moments, days, months, and even years of darkness and light, again and again, forgetting and re-membering, forgetting and remembering. My point is, between our (re)defining moments, which always bring with them the light of remembrance, there will be periods of darkness when we go totally unconscious and forget who we are—and that's okay. The practice is to work toward staying conscious in the tunnels, knowing that the light is just ahead. This practice requires our attention *and* intention. This is the pathway of our personal evolution as well as the entry point to our (re)defining moments. The more we evolve in our understanding of who we really are, the fewer tunnels we shall have to pass through on the sojourn back to the authentic self.

Remembering and Forgetting
Requires Knowing and Unknowing

This was a lesson I originally learned back in 1977 when I first stumbled onto the pathway of mindful living. I recall what my teacher said to my classmates and me as we were celebrating the completion of our first year of classes in practical spirituality. He admonished us to not get too puffed up about what we had learned, and for good reason. He said, and I paraphrase: ultimately, following the path of awakening is a lifelong process of knowing and unknowing again and again as you grow. It's a process of remembering and forgetting what you know, and remembering it again. It is a cycle that is as eternal as life itself. You entered this life not knowing anything but already seeking something, and through your willingness to go from unknowing to knowing, as from darkness into the light, you have begun to remember who you really are. But alas, as sure as night also follows day, you shall forget it again and again as you continue your journey. Be assured, though, that if you stay the course, you shall remember again and again as well.

The lesson for my classmates and me so many years ago wasn't about information, facts, and figures we had once known but since forgotten—it was a remembrance of who we truly are and had always been. The educational process wasn't about adding anything new to our minds; it was actually about removing erroneous thoughts and beliefs we had collected along life's journey that were covering over something quite wonderful that had always been there, our authentic self. The irony is that we must awaken to the idea that it is only through our willingness to repeatedly enter into unknowingness that we are able to continue to seek the light to be found in knowing our truth. Isn't that an amazing paradox? We have to enter into unknowing to discover the truth, because there is no room for unknowing in a mind that believes it already knows the truth!

It really requires a willingness to come to the edge of all we think (there is the landmine) we "know" and then free-fall

into our unknowing in absolute faith. Sometimes our thinking gets in the way of our faith. The faith to which I am referring is also known as divine surrender—total and complete
abandonment of the thinking mind and surrender to the sacred
heart. It's in that very instant of divine surrender that remembrance of who we really are begins to arise, once again from
our center, to the surface of our lives. It's an amazing process
to behold because in the journey of remembering who we truly
are, whatever information (knowing) and methodology (action)
we need to unfold ourselves seems to show up right at the
time we need it.

What We Are Really Looking For

One of the "tunnels of forgetfulness" where many of us tend to
get derailed happens when we misinterpret our wants for our
needs. The pathway back to living an authentic life is lined with
many very seductive wants—things that have little to do with
who we *really* are. No doubt many of our wants are very difficult
to bypass, nor should they have to be bypassed—as long as we
are clear that what we "have" in no way defines who we are.
Many of our lives are unknowingly defined by our "wants,"
which often, driven by the egoic-self, push us further away from
the authentic self. This is a misguided quest because the one
thing our soul *truly desires* will never be found in the world of
our wants. Remember, to a large degree, where we focus our
primary attention determines what defines us. So let us be clear
not to confuse our *wants* with our *needs*. The practice is to be
mindful of the difference between the two. In his "Hierarchy of

Needs," Abraham Maslow speaks to some of the inherent essential needs for survival that every human being has a desire and right to pursue, such as the following:

- Air to breathe
- Clean water
- Adequate food
- A safe shelter and living environment
- Good health
- Law and order
- Belongingness and a sense of connection to others
- Love, self-esteem, and a sense of purpose
- Personal fulfillment through self-actualization

Fulfilling our needs does not define who we are, but it does serve us well on the journey to wholeness. Beyond our intrinsic needs, most of us have a litany of things on our "want list" that can easily become the baseline by which we mistakenly define ourselves. Some of our wants are more base or fundamental to achieving an enhanced lifestyle, while others are more esoteric, emotional, or even spiritually driven. In all cases, however, on the sojourn back to the authentic self, the question that we are compelled to ask is, Does the fulfillment of my wants have anything to do with how I define myself or how I am defined in the world? Below is an example of what someone might say they "want." See if you can relate to any of these:

- Perfect weather
- For my children to always act appropriately
- The perfect partner who completes and fulfills me

- A beautiful, trim, sexy body that doesn't look its age—ever
- For others to believe what I believe, politically and spiritually
- More (than enough) money
- A bigger big-screen television
- A better car
- A more successful career
- A bigger, more luxurious home
- A political system that functions well
- Harmony among the world's religions
- World peace
- Or _____ (fill in the blank)

Did you find any of your wants on this list? If you are like me, more than likely you did. Notice that not all wants appear to be self-serving, but they actually are because we think when they are achieved, we will have found what we are looking for. Have you guessed yet what that might be? The bottom line is, we don't really want any of these things. We desire what lies several layers beneath them. With a little bit of self-inquiry, we can begin asking ourselves what the deeper desire is behind many of our wants that makes them so compelling.

As an example of how to personalize this self-inquiry process, I had a conversation with myself I will share with you: I thought to myself, *If I managed to manifest my favorite want as a reality in my life today, how would that make me feel in comparison to how I actually feel right now? In other words, how would fulfilling that want alter my life?* The immediate answer was, *I would be happier.* Knowing that, underlying the one just answered, another question was waiting in the wings, I replied to myself, *And how will*

you feel when your happiness around this fulfilled want eventually dis-
sipates, which it surely will, because that is what always happens when
your happiness is contingent on the acquisition of your wants? You know
they are temporal at best and that new wants will continue to float to the
surface, yes? (This is when the theory of "hedonic adaptation"
kicks in, which is sometimes referred to as the "hedonic treadmill" because it describes the relentless and endless pursuit of
"things" that entice us today, but once acquired, become just
another thing we feel indifference toward, which leads us to
pursue the "next" thing. . . . It's a treadmill most of us can identify with.) Feeling a bit frustrated with this self-dialogue, I said
to myself, *Fine . . . spare me the lecture and just tell me what it is I*
really desire under all these fleeting wants. The answer was so clear,
so concise, and so gentle, it was palpable and could not be
mistaken: *inner peace. What you really desire is the inner peace that*
comes without conditions attached.

> "Nothing can bring peace but the revelation of the individual
> to himself, and a recognition of his direct relationship to the
> Universe."
>
> —ERNEST HOLMES

Most of us are not even consciously aware that we long for inner
peace but, beyond our basic hierarchy of needs, behind every
want we have, is the deep desire to *experience* the feeling of deep
inner peace. Period. The "mystery desire" behind all our wants
is to feel at peace in the moment, regardless of what is. The mistaken belief is that once our wants are fulfilled, *then* we will be
all right . . . *then* we'll be safe . . . *then* we'll be loved . . . *then*
we'll be included . . . *then* we'll be respected . . . *then* we'll be
secure in the world . . . *then* we will be happy. There it is. What

we really desire is so elegantly simple—inner peace, the peace that passes all understanding. The only problem is, when we seek inner peace through the fulfillment of our wants, we step right back onto that treadmill. There will always be another "then" we have to deal with first. The practice is to be conscious enough, when our "want list" arises in our mind (and it will, and that's okay), to see beyond the want and touch base with the deeper wisdom self within—our authentic self. It knows the difference between our wants and needs. Ask yourself, *Do I need this* _____ (fill in the blank)*, or do I want it?* Then notice how your attachment to your wants often causes some degree of suffering because there is a place in you beyond the self-gratifying ego that knows, even before you get it, it will never be enough. In other words, at some level, you know it separates you from who you really are and the source from which you came. The good news is, if you are even the slightest bit awake, you'll also see the light of a (re)defining moment coming just around the bend.

A Trip to the Far Country
Can Lead to a (Re)Defining Moment

"It may be the satisfaction I need depends on my going away,
so that when I've gone and come back, I'll find it at home."
—RUMI

Never let it be said that our (re)defining moments only come gift-wrapped in blue skies, sunshine, and green lights on the pathway to a life worth living. Sometimes a road trip to the far country is not necessarily a bad thing if it helps us remember who we were born to be. The great teacher Jesus eloquently illustrated a (re)defining moment (and the importance of remembering who we really are) in his parable of the Prodigal Son (Luke 15:11–32). The story tells of a farmer who had two sons. The younger son (the "prodigal son") was discontent with life on the farm and asked his father for his inheritance so he could hit the road and see what lay in the far country, hoping for a new and more exciting life. His father, being unconditionally loving, gave his son his inheritance, and off the young man went, leaving his father and older, stay-at-home brother behind. Once in the far country, the son squandered his inheritance, living in a less-than-mindful manner (a.k.a., "wild living"), to a point where he found himself penniless and working for a local farmer mucking the pig pens and eating the pigs' food just to survive. Then, one day, he realized that even the hired workers on his father's farm had it better than he did. He decided to return home and ask his father for forgiveness. Of course, the unconditionally loving father met him with open arms and reinstated him to his rightful place in the family with all its benefits and privileges, and all was well—sort of. The prodigal son's return didn't sit well with the older, stay-at-home son who had grown completely unaware of the good life he had by staying on the farm where all his needs were met. Because of his total lack of awareness of how blessed his life *already* was, he became filled with resentment, jealousy, and discontentment over his brother's graceful reentry into the family. At this point, the father points out to the elder son that his good had always been there, *right in front of him*—he simply needed to awaken and see and accept his good. Thus ends the story.

The moral of this parable is difficult to miss. While it abounds with idioms and metaphor, the power in this story is that it is our story. At times, we have all been the prodigal son (or daughter) separating ourselves from the source of our good (the Original Self), which Jesus referred to as the Father. The quest of the prodigal son leads us on a path to the far country—a place of separation and forgetfulness in which we find ourselves whenever we are seduced by the power of our wants. As a result, the farther we wander into the far country, the more we distance ourselves from an awareness of who we really are. The journey to the far country is fueled by the belief that "there" is better than "here," and that when we arrive "there," the conditions will be more to our liking, which, in turn, will cause us to feel more at peace with ourselves. As he soon found out, the prodigal son discovered that the "there" (living in the far country) ultimately spawned the feeling and experience of separation between him and his father and, because of it, he suffered. In other words, he wasn't all that peaceful once he ran out of the coin of the realm. This is simply a variation on a theme based on the theory of hedonic adaptation. His (re)defining moment in the far country came while living and dining among the swine. At what appeared to be the darkest moment of his life, his memory kicked in, the "light" went on, and he came out of the metaphoric tunnel knowing who he really was and from where he had come.

> "When he came to his senses, he said, 'How many of my father's hired servants have food to spare, and here I am starving to death! I will set out and go back to my father . . .'"
> —LUKE 15:17–18

Healing that sense of separation was easy—all he had to do was remember where he came from, rise, and return home where his father awaited him with unconditional love. Again, this is our story. The moment we consciously recall our personal relationship and unity with the Original Self, It awaits us with open arms. Lesson learned: life is better at home than in the far country. What mattered was his *remembering* the way home and starting the journey back. That is what (re)defining moments do. When things appear the darkest, if we come to our senses and remember the Source with which we are one, everything changes. We were born in the womb of the One—the Source of all that makes life worth living, and just like the prodigal son, it is our divine birthright.

Becoming Who We Were Born to Be Is a Return to Wholeness through the Portal of a (Re)Defining Moment

To remember the source from which we came is the act of coming back to the Whole; returning to our original state of Grace. This is what the story of the prodigal son points out; it's a return to wholeness made possible by a (re)defining moment. Ultimately, living with the swine and eating their food helped him realize a "peace" was missing from his life. He realized that all his *needs* were met right there at home, but his *wants* had mesmerized him and led him to the far country. It was only after he "came to his senses" by remembering who he was born to be that he set out on the path home to reintegrate with the wholeness from which he came. It is easy to be seduced by the call of the far country because it seems to be the way of the world, which essentially defines itself from the outside in rather than the inside out. That does not mean it has to be our chosen way. Taking an occasional road trip to the far country is not necessar-

ily a bad thing; it can, in and of itself, provide (re)defining moments. What matters most is *remembering* the way home—and
that is what our (re)defining moments are all about. They point
the way home.

POINTS TO PONDER AND PERSONALIZE

- Can you relate with my experience on the bullet train,
  repeatedly going through the metaphoric dark tunnels
  and back into the light, forgetting and remembering
  your connectedness to something infinitely larger than
  yourself? The practice is, while in the tunnel, not to
  deny it by going unconscious. Stay connected and mindful, and accept that you are in the tunnel—and have
  faith that as you continue to move "forward," you are
  actually finding your way "back" to the your authentic
  self, that the light needed to get you there is already
  burning brightly.

- Do you ever find yourself on the "hedonic treadmill,"
  thinking that the next want fulfilled will yield the happiness you dream of? Remember, the desire that underlies every want you have is really the desire for inner
  peace, the desire to feel whole and complete in every
  moment. Think of inner peace as an inherent *need* you
  have rather than a want. If you go back and review
  Maslow's Hierarchy of Needs, you'll notice that when
  all your innate needs are successfully met and combined,
  the result will naturally be inner peace.

- It's important not to demonize your wants—they are a normal and appropriate part of the human experience. Seeking and fulfilling your wants in life is not a bad thing—it's a great thing! The practice is to be certain that you are not defining yourself by what you have or don't have, accumulate or don't accumulate, accomplish or don't accomplish during your life but rather by the person you bring to the planet, an individuated spark of the Original Self.

- Can you see any part of the prodigal son (or daughter) in yourself? If so, perhaps it's time to realize you may have been living in the far country too long. Have you forgotten the truth about yourself and slipped into spiritual amnesia, not remembering the Source from which you came? The good news is, it's never too late to return home.

- The second part of the story of the prodigal son involves the "stay-at-home son" who was oblivious to the good that was already all around him on the farm; his *every* need was fulfilled, and he didn't even realize it. Can you see any part of yourself in the stay-at-home son? Consider exploring where the tendency to take things for granted may be showing up in your life today. In the case of either son, as Dorothy declared in *The Wizard of Oz*, "There's no place like home." Coming home is a journey well worth taking. Are you on board?

CHAPTER 4

Ten Road Signs That a (Re)Defining Moment Lies Ahead

The Practice of Mindfulness Opens the Portal

Slow down and enjoy life. It's not only the scenery you miss by going fast—you also miss the sense of where you are going and why.

—EDDIE CANTOR

When I was eighteen years old, driving my beefed-up '57 Chevy always seemed to put me in another world. With its oversized, big-block engine and close-ratio quick-shifting four on the floor, custom paint, and wide tires, it was a thing of beauty and power. Unfortunately, the state of mind I was often in when driving it was not necessarily a mindful one. If, as a teen, you ever had the chance to drive a high-powered car, you know what I mean. Add a high dose of testosterone to the mix, and the stupid in you can come out very quickly. Let's just say, speeding was hard to avoid. Late one evening on the way home from a date, while driving around a curve at a (much) higher rate of speed than I should have been going, I ran an unexpected stop sign and was pulled over by a sheriff. Admittedly, I was not paying attention to my driving because, beyond having a lead foot, I was far too busy singing along with the Beatles. While I wasn't thrilled about it at the time, I knew I had no grounds for arguing the ticket and, truthfully, it was a great lesson for me—it could have been a lot worse. To this day, I still remember what the officer said as he handed me the ticket: "You were very fortunate this time because no one got hurt. If you were driving slower and paying more attention, you would have seen the bright yellow Caution sign about a hundred yards back where the road begins to curve, warning you that there was a stop sign ahead. Next time, slow down and pay more attention to the signs . . . and you may live to see twenty."

Little did I know it at the time, but receiving that traffic ticket marked what, years later, became a (re)defining moment for me. How so? At the time, this was not a lesson that stuck with me very long; however, it must have sunk in at a deeper level because, over the years, the importance of that experience has resurfaced repeatedly in countless ways and times. It's probably one of the primary reasons I am still here. The message about slowing down has become the overall theme for my life. To this day, often when I see someone driving fast or recklessly, that memory is triggered and it helps me see how easy it is for one's mind and body to be in two different places at the same time—a precursor to a "wreck" of some sort in life. The takeaway here is, in the process of finding our way back to the authentic self, if we are not *mindfully* watching for them, we will often miss the signs along the way telling us a (re)defining moment is at hand. (Re)defining moments always create an opening for us to see a little deeper into who we really are *if* we are willing to slow down and notice them.

Mindfulness Brings Our
Beingness into Our Doingness

SLOWING DOWN IS A MINDFULNESS PRACTICE ONE CAN DO ANYTIME AND ANY PLACE

Right now, if you intentionally take a deep breath and focus on that breath, you will discover that your mind and your body are in the same place at the same time. The irony is, our body can't be any place other than in the present moment, but far too often, our mind is elsewhere. Mindfulness is the practice of calling the thinking mind back to where the body is, wherein the two become as one in the present moment. As you incorporate your awareness of being present in the moment, your *doing* (the "who" you are) becomes infused with your *being* (the "what" you are) as the activity at hand. At this level of mindful living, your every action becomes a portal for a potential (re)defining moment, be it while driving the car, mowing the lawn, changing the baby's diaper, selling real estate, performing brain surgery, or making love to your significant other. The primary thing is to be present with what you are doing, and you'll be amazed by what is revealed to you. Even if you are unaware of it at the time, every experience you have in life holds the possibility of being a (re)defining moment. If you are not mindfully open to and present in the moment, however, that possibility will pass you by faster than my '57 Chevy zipped through that stop sign. The practice is to slow down and mindfully watch for the signs that tell you a (re)defining moment is just around the bend.

Ten Signs That You Are
Approaching a (Re)Defining Moment

As with all circumstances we encounter along the pathway to a life worth living, there are lessons we can learn from our current experiences. It requires the ability to "freeze-frame" our life, or stand back and become a conscious observer of our own thoughts, feelings, and actions, noticing where they are taking us. When you set your *intention* to consciously evolve, you naturally begin to pay *attention* and (re)defining moments appear as they are needed. They are drawn to you sequentially to support you in the process of staying the course on your pilgrimage, each one a perfectly aligned portal in space and time, opening and closing, creating whatever experience is required to guide you back to an awareness of your authentic self where you began the journey. While the possible circumstances that preclude a (re)defining moment are limitless, here are my top ten signs to watch for. Remember, the practice is to slow down and mindfully watch for these signs and, when they pop up, stay engaged in the moment rather than zipping past them on to another distraction.

1. Moments that challenge your ego and moments that your ego challenges you.

Have you ever been emotionally wounded by something you or someone else said or did that embarrassed, diminished, humiliated, or angered you? Conversely, have you ever taken your "awesomeness" a bit too much for granted by getting a little puffed up, actually believing you are the collective personification of all things wonderful that certain others (including yourself) might say you are? Knowing you are human, most likely the answer to these questions is "yes." In all these scenarios, the aforementioned reactions draw their life force from the pugnacious behavior of the egoic-self (a surface dweller), whose sole job it is to keep you diverted from ever connecting with your authentic self.

Many people unknowingly allow their entire life to be defined by their ego because they are not aware that the ego is even on the job, or they are simply not willing to challenge it. The practice is to be conscious and present in the moment long enough to identify and examine certain feelings that arise and, when they do, challenge them. Ask yourself, What is the source of this anger, embarrassment, or humiliation? What is the source of this puffed-up, overzealous, full-of-myself attitude? Certainly it is not coming from the depths of the authentic self. This is not about demonizing the ego; it's about putting it in its proper place and taking back the power you have bestowed upon it to fool you into believing it has anything to do with the true source of your power or identity.

The action of mindfully slowing down and having that conversation with your self will momentarily open the door to a (re)defining moment—allowing you a deeper look into who you really are at your center, far beyond what the ego has to say. How will you know you are talking to your authentic self rather than the ego? The authentic self will never lead you to believe that you have anything to defend, prove, or be puffed up about, because your true identity is not determined by what your ego or the world has to say about you. It is impossible for your authentic self to ever be embarrassed, humiliated, angered, or puffed up because it takes nothing personal—ever. So watch for those moments when your ego shows up to pout, defend, or gloat over what is going on in the moment, and slow down. If you are mindful, a (re)defining moment may by just ahead.

2. Unexpected events.

There can be little doubt that events such as the terrorist attacks of September 11, 2001, and other tragic events since then can be (re)defining moments, not just for those personally involved but for an entire country or even the world. September 11 gave us all a reason to slow down and take a deep look within. Unexpected events such as an emergency can open the portal for a (re)defining moment in a heartbeat because they cause us to draw upon on our innate wisdom that supersedes our intellect— an emergency instantly connects us to that place deep within that knows what needs to be done and how to do it. While this may not always be the case, if you have ever been forced to act during an emergency, you might have experienced everything slowing down—as if it were a slow-motion scene in a movie. You know you are not physically slowing down, but if you can remain *conscious and present in the moment* of an emergency, you'll witness the fact that you are merging with your center within that is tremendously powerful . . . and it knows how to do what needs to be done in that moment.

The practice is to remember that, far beyond the time when the crisis ends, that center of inner peace and power is still there. It never went anywhere, and it has always been there. You just may not have not been *consciously* aware of its presence. Perhaps an unexpected event such as an emergency can open the portal to a (re)defining moment and allow you to take the vertical dive, going from the chaos on the surface of life to the center of your being, where you are reminded that the authentic self is present.

3. Times of significant loss.

Unexpected as they might be, (re)defining moments are always lingering just on the other side of significant loss, regardless of what the loss is. It could be the loss of a partner to death or divorce, the perceived loss of the family unit due to the empty nest syndrome, or the death of a child or parent or pet. Perhaps it's the loss of a job or a title, financial status, home, reputation . . . or even the loss of your, or a loved one's, current health. The point is, any *significant* loss puts you on the precipice of a (re)defining moment. Many people have unknowingly defined themselves based on the status of one or more of the aforementioned things: once that person or thing is gone, so, too, is how they have defined themselves. While the loss of any the aforementioned may indeed be tragic and worthy of concern or grieving, none of them represent who *you* really are; rather, they represent experiences that are always subject to transition in your life. Who you really are is not subject to transition because the true Self is formless and changeless.

If you are mindful, at the appropriate time, doing some self-inquiry (to be more fully discussed in Sign #10) in the aftermath of significant loss can open the portal to a (re)defining moment, allowing you to plumb the depths of the question, *Who am I, beyond being a spouse or partner, a single person, a mother, an employee, a job title, a bank account status, or a preferred physical condition? Without these things, who am I really?* If you are mindfully and sincerely willing to still your mind and ask that question in silence, you will receive the answer. This can be a (re)defining moment when you remember that the authentic self is never diminished by the comings and goings of the human condition. As long as you live in a human skin, you will experience significant loss of some sort at some time or another. It's not a choice; it's a matter of how you choose to frame the loss. With the proper perspective, you may find a (re)defining moment at hand. When those times happen, the practice is to slow down and remember that who you truly are can *never* be defined in human terms or by the human condition; the Original Self from which you came is always there, waiting to embrace you in times of loss—*always*.

4. First-time experiences.

Can you remember your first day of school, your first job, your first date, the first time you drove a car, your first relationship after a previous long-term relationship ended via death or divorce, or even the first time you ate something new and foreign to your palate? Whether you knew it or not, that was a (re)defining moment for you because it added another notch in your belt as an evolving being. You expanded, you moved, from one place of comfort and relative certainty and into, albeit for a brief time, a new role that forced you to go deeper into the unexplored territory of your sense of self. In short, you went from unknowing to knowing. I remember my first day on the first "official" job I ever had. At twelve years of age, I was hired as a shoeshine boy in a barbershop and went into "business" for myself. I had never dealt with money or total strangers before, but when I put on that apron for the first time and shined my first pair of shoes—and was *actually paid* a whole thirty-five cents—a surge of energy moved in me and I felt something I had never felt before. While I had no idea at the time, I had just experienced a (re)defining moment—I had discovered a new part of myself I didn't know existed. In that moment, I had become a willing participant in expanding my place in the world and the role I would choose to play in it.

The point is, as you evolve in your understanding of *your* unique place in the world, remember you were born hardwired to express—to expand and explore unknown territory by drawing upon the vast resources of your authentic self. Even if you are not aware that you are drawing upon those resources, that is exactly what you are doing. The key is to awaken to that fact. When you *mindfully* enter the door of a new first-time experience, you'll notice the portal to a (re)defining moment directly ahead because you are adding depth, substance, and form to the "what" you are, showing up as the "who" you are. In other words, you have taken the vertical plunge and brought the authentic self up and into the horizontal life. The practice is to slow down and savor the experience while it lasts because, if you are intentionally growing, yet another new first-time experience is coming directly around the bend. The only question is, will you see it when it shows up? Such is the evolving journey of finding your way back to your authentic self—mindfulness matters.

5. Discontentment.

Discontentment is defined as "dissatisfaction with one's current circumstances." Many people are defined by their current circumstances because they don't pay attention to their discontentment, or they manage it in an unhealthy manner, one way or another, suppressing it, diverting it, or simply pretending it's not there. When you consciously make the connection between your discontentment and your innate desire to evolve, it becomes "divine" discontentment. Do you recall, in chapter 2, the discussion regarding the power of unexpressed energy—that energetic impulse, nudging you to push out (or express)? Discontentment is often where that nudge begins. Because the tendency is to resist change and, therefore, growth, sometimes discontentment expresses (disguises) itself as restlessness, addictions, resentment, unhappiness, and misguided actions—or, if ignored long enough, the opposite: boredom, disengagement, resignation, and lethargy.

If you are experiencing any of these symptoms, you would be well served to pay attention to them. It is quite possible that underneath your discontentment with what "is," the authentic self is knocking, inviting you to explore what "can be." Discontentment is very much like a red flare directed inward rather than skyward—it signals to your mind that a (re)defining moment is actually seeking you; it is inviting you to not just slow down, but to stop and *mindfully* consider the opportunity at hand. Discontentment offers a ripe and juicy opportunity to consciously evolve if you are open to doing something proactive when the moment arises rather than grouse about it or ignore it. Being dissatisfied with the current circumstances and doing something about it are two very different things: making a conscious choice to move from what is to what can be, no doubt, *is* a (re)defining moment in the making. Just slow down and watch for the signal flares. Discontentment really can be divine if you pay appropriate attention to its nudge.

6. Disappointment.

No one is immune to disappointment. The question is, how will you choose to allow it to affect you? Disappointment can be the passageway that leads to discouragement, frustration, and failure . . . *or* to a (re)defining moment that is beckoning you to discover who you really are and move forward. The choice is yours. In his inspiring book, *The Last Lecture*, Randy Pausch writes, "The brick walls are there for a reason. The brick walls are not there to keep us out. The brick walls are there to give us a chance to show how badly we want something . . . the brick walls are there to stop the people who don't want it badly enough. They're there to stop the other people."

History is filled with examples of individuals who, in the pursuit of their dreams, aspirations, and goals, hit the brick wall Pausch is describing and were stopped dead in their tracks, having initially failed in their mission. The reason they are recorded in the annals of history is not because they initially failed, however; they are remembered because they stayed the course and ultimately succeeded. They found a way to get past the brick wall—they dug under, climbed over, went around, or broke through it. They chose not to be defeated or defined by their failure because they didn't get stuck in the muck and mire of their disappointment. Instead, they used their disappointment as a base to dig deeper into the core of their true character and find a part of themselves they didn't know existed. The manner in which they dealt with their disappointment became a portal to a (re)defining moment.

No doubt, at some point, you and every other person on the planet has been dealt a blow that brought on a feeling of disappointment. Somehow the expectations you held for something wonderful may have had a head-on collision with a brick wall, perhaps leaving you feeling destitute, alone, sad, and deeply frustrated. If you are mindful, and have the right perspective, you can refocus your life's disappointments as the entry point to a (re)defining moment. This is the perfect example of the difference between living "horizontally" on the surface of life and being defined by conditions, and taking the vertical dive to the center of our being wherein the authentic self awaits, with the "soul-ution" to our disappointment. When the next disappointment pops up on your pathway to the life of your dreams—and it will at some point—slow down and, rather than getting stuck, allow yourself time to dig deep and connect with that creative, tireless genius within who knows how to get past the brick wall. If you are mindful, your biggest disappointments can be a precursor to a (re)defining moment just ahead. The operative words here are *if you are mindful*. Perspective really is everything when it comes to our (re)defining moments.

7. Experiencing someone or something that instantly inspires you to grow.

There are multiple definitions for the word *inspiration*. The one that most resonates with me is, "A divine influence directly and immediately exerted upon the mind or soul." The operative words here are *directly and immediately*. A direct experience can never really be fully described or shared with another because it is innately personal—and you'll know when you have one because it immediately reveals itself to you *if* you are present in the moment and open to the experience. I mention this because when I was twenty-eight years old, I had such a moment of inspiration, and it became perhaps the greatest single (re)defining moment of my entire life. I had recently entered what I would now call my darkest night of the soul. My life was metaphorically on fire. Having just gone through a very nasty divorce while, at the same time, also coming to grips with the fact that I was in a career that was slowly sucking the life force out me, I was desperately unhappy. It is safe to say I didn't at all like where I was in life and who I perceived myself to be.

One night while sitting alone watching a baseball game on television, I began my normal ritual of channel surfing during the commercial break. On the very next channel, there appeared an impeccably dressed man, sitting calmly at a desk, talking about me! I don't mean me personally, but he was speaking directly *to* me as if he knew exactly what I was going through at that moment. He hooked me, so I listened intently to the rest of his program. His name was Dr. Frank Richelieu, and the wisdom of his words penetrated every fiber of my being. I say this because, within the first ten minutes of listening to him, the fire within that had been consuming me was immediately extinguished. I was so inspired, I was on the phone the next day learning more about the teaching he espoused. It has been said that when the student is ready, the teacher appears. A teacher is one who inspires others to grow into their own full potential. I guess I was really ready for my teacher because in the years that followed, Dr. Richelieu became my mentor and friend, guiding me to a new career and life that has led me to the path I walk today. No doubt, clicking that remote control entirely changed the direction of my life. It opened an unexpected portal for what would become one of the greatest (re)defining moments of my life. I will be forever grateful that, for some reason, in that exact moment, I was *slowly* clicking the remote control—just slow enough to linger on a few words that hooked me and would forever change my life. Have you ever connected with someone or something that inspired you, but rather than pause and explore why you were inspired, you let the moment pass you by? As I said, when the student is ready, the teacher appears, *but* the student has to be awake enough to recognize the opportunity and seize it before such a (re)defining moment passes by.

(Re)defining moments don't happen only in times of desperation, when one's life is on fire; they can happen at any time and any place, including in the best of times. The practice is to be mindful enough to know when your teachers appear so you don't miss them. How can you identify your teachers? For one thing, they will never point to themselves as the source of your well-being or connection to your authentic self. Instead, they will point you inward. Your teachers might include not just adults, but also children and other sources you may not normally think of as teachers—all of whom command your *immediate* attention. It could be as simple as a breathtaking sunset, trees as they gently bend with the wind, or your dog joyfully romping at play or resting peacefully. The list of possible teachers who can inspire us is endless. The telltale sign that such a person or thing has entered the arena of your life as a teacher is an immediate sense of inspiration; it's an intuitive knowing that there is more to know about *your* life and who *you* really are. All you need to do is slow down and pay attention to the "nudge" when you feel it—and when you do, you will receive the lesson if you are teachable.

8. Birth of a loved one.

I distinctly remember the moment nearly three decades ago when, standing in the delivery room, the doctor placed my newborn daughter in my arms. As I gazed deeply into the dark pool of her just-opened eyes, something moved in me that forever altered my perception of the miracle and mystery of life and the role it was to play in my future. After wiping away my tears, I realized that what I had just experienced was a (re)defining moment—it entirely changed the direction and meaning of my life at two levels. While I didn't fully understand it at the time, in a heartbeat, who I had thought myself to be until that moment was being challenged: in a linear fashion, instantly, new definitions such as *father, protector, provider, teacher, role model, future T-ball coach,* and many others came flooding in. Yet at the same time, a deeper knowing, beyond words, moved through me, affirming that underneath these newly self-imposed labels, as wonderful as they were, lay a quiet presence that knew nothing about labels I had yet to discover. My experience in the delivery room was transformational because I walked out of that delivery room door a different person from who I was when I walked in. It was among the first of many singular moments in my life when, metaphorically, an invisible door would be flung open at the most unexpected time and through which I would step, only to find deeper parts of myself.

Perhaps you are currently at a point in your life where you have already seen how the birth of a loved one can be a (re)defining moment for you. If so, the practice is to slow down and revisit your memories of that event and allow them to remind you of how, in that moment, you discovered parts of yourself you had no idea were there. This is the mystery and magic of true (re)defining moments—they live within us forever and, thus, we are forever changed by them. Remembering to remember those moments is the key. Perhaps the birth of a loved one is an experience that still awaits you in the future. Just know that when that time comes, a (re)defining moment is fast on its heels. Remember to slow down so you don't miss it, and be in awe of what you see and experience. It will alter your view of yourself and life forever.

9. Death of a loved one—or your own death.

The coming and going of one's life is a topic that affects us all. We live in an infinite Universe that is the essence of eternal life and, therefore, it is not life that comes and goes—it's our bodies that do. Most of us are good with the "coming" part—it's the "going" part that we tend to avoid thinking about. This is a topic that deserves our attention, however, because it is one that every one of us will have an opportunity to experience at some point; it is only a matter of when. Many people are terrified to discuss death because they have not made peace with leaving this world, but with a deepened perspective, it is possible to see the death of a loved one, or our own pending death, as containing the potential for a (re)defining moment.

Processing the death of a loved one *is* a process. Whether it is a sudden and unexpected transition or one you see coming due to prolonged illness or declining health, to contemplate the meaning of life without that person opens the sacred door to the heart and invites you to explore several things. First, you get to fully appreciate the role that person played in your life, be it a parent, a child, a close family member, or your best friend, as well as to grieve their passing and the loss they represent in your life. Second, if you are willing, you'll be able to objectively discern to what degree your life has been defined by that relationship. In other words, regardless of how wonderful they may or may not have been, you'll see how much of your identity may have been wrapped up in that person. This is particularly true for those who lose longtime spouses or partners. When you have spent a large portion of your life with another person, it's quite easy to lose your identity in them because "I" understandably tends to become "we."

The question is, when "we" ends, whether it be with a spouse, a child, or any other close association, how will you define yourself? If you are mindful, when you lose a loved one, you will know that the portal for a (re)defining moment will appear when you are ready to embrace it. When a loved one dies, beyond the shock, sadness, and grieving, there lies the emptiness of a void that can never be filled. In the spaciousness of enough time, however, you will see that the best way to honor that relationship is to reenter and mindfully engage in life, knowing that you are not less because of that loss. In fact, you are more because you carry the imprint of that person's essence in your expanded heart. The practice is to remember that while you carry their memory in you, they are not you and, therefore, did not then and do not now define the essence of the unique individual you are. It is then that you will know that the passing of that loved one can be the marker for a (re)defining moment because not only are you clear on the impact that person had on your life, you also have the opportunity to explore and find deeper parts of yourself possibly unknown until now. This is what (re)defining moments do—they allow you to uncover (or *re*discover) that unique part of *yourself* you may have lost sight of, your authentic self.

> "There is no need to be afraid of death. It is not the end of the
> physical body that should worry us. Rather, our concern must
> be to *live* while we are alive—to release our inner selves from

the spiritual death that comes with living behind a facade
designed to conform to external definitions of who and what
we are . . . to the extent that we become captives of culturally
defined role expectations and behaviors—stereotypes, not
ourselves—we block our capacity for self-actualization. We
interfere with becoming all that we can be."
                                    —ELISABETH KÜBLER-ROSS,
                              Death: The Final Stage of Growth

When it comes to your own "going," it has been said that living
a fully conscious life can only be surpassed by dying a fully conscious death. Someone suggested that it's wise to live every day
as if it were your last because one day you'll be right. Here is a
question to ponder: if you knew you had only a very limited
amount of time to live, what might you do differently today
than you did yesterday? I suspect—and hope—you might let go
of much emotional baggage. You would most likely take more
time to "smell the roses" and less time pushing an agenda that
creates stress. Your calendar might become less important than
the moment right in front of you. You might begin to appreciate
your partner and family far *more*, and take them for granted far
less. If you made those changes today and took them seriously
rather than waiting for your final days, don't you think your life
would become a sacred continuum of (re)defining moments?
Regardless of the timing, be it seven days or seventy years from
now, there is still that place within you that will always know
the true essence of who you are and were born to be. Dying a
conscious death is perhaps the ultimate (re)defining moment because it takes you back to the place where you began the journey, the Original Self. Slowing down will help you see that even
in your own passing, there are (re)defining moments yet to be
experienced.

10. Asking the big questions.

It has been said that our personal growth and evolution is generally motivated by either inspiration or desperation. In either
case, if you have a predisposition to self-inquiry, you'll find your
(re)defining moments popping up in a delightful way. Sincere
self-inquiry is taking the vertical path directly from living on the
surface of life to the center of your being. When you courageously and earnestly ask yourself the big questions that require
you to dig deep, the deeper you dig, the closer you get to merging with your true self. How will you know the answers you
receive are correct? They will lead to actions that honor Life;
they will be answers that put you on a course of action that
harms no one, including yourself; that affirms the presence of a
prevailing power for good that lies within you that guides, pro-
tects, and sustains you; and seeks only the highest and best for
you and every sentient being. They will be answers that move
you forward on the pathway to your wholeness as a fulfilled and
joyfully self-expressed person. Most important, they will be
answers that connect your mind and heart with your soul.

What are some of the big questions that often precede a (re)de-
fining moment? Here is a list for starters. You can add to it ac-
cording to your own inner compass.

> Who am I?
> Why am I?
> Where did I come from?
> Where will I go when I leave here?
> Why can't I let _____ (fill in the blank) go?

What role do I play in how my life is unfolding?

Am I being who I was born to be?

Am I learning from my mistakes and failures and
growing every day because of them?

Have I been looking to someone (or something) for
my sense of identity?

Am I living a life of purpose and meaning?

When I die, will the planet be a better place than it
was when I got here—because I was here?

What are my gifts I bring to share with the world,
and am I sharing them—and if not, why?

Be assured, asking the right questions with clear intention and a willingness to faithfully follow where they lead you requires courage because once you ask the question, you have to be willing to dance with the answer, which may or may not be to your liking. If you stay on the dance floor and embrace the answers you receive, however, you'll find yourself on the pathway back to your authentic self. The practice is to remember to slow down and "be" with your questions in real time—don't rush the process. Not only will your answers that already exist within you be revealed, you also will have automatically pushed the "reset" button on that which defines you. When you make a conscious choice to ask yourself the big questions, it alters your perception, which in turn alters your behavior, which in turn alters your experience. With that level of awareness, all life becomes a quest leading you back to the place you never really left—your oneness with the Original Self, which, in truth, you are now and have *always* been. Make no doubt about it, be it motivated by either inspiration or desperation, asking the big questions opens the portal to a (re)defining moment that will reshape your entire life in a profound way.

Points to Ponder and Personalize

- Can you relate to the idea that your mind can be just like my '57 Chevy, driving so fast you are zipping past many (re)defining moments that could truly alter the course of your life? Mindfulness is about intentionally slowing down your mind when it is zooming way out in front of you and calling it back to where your body is in any given moment. In the process, you will be far more likely to see the signs (opportunities) that lie directly in front of you, inviting you to stop and find a part of yourself you may have long forgotten about. Slowing down your mind is a wise and powerful way to recognize that any and every moment might be the entry point to a (re)defining moment.

- If you take time to equally explore the ten signposts preceding a possible (re)defining moment, you may discover exactly which ones you need to pay special attention to. The more time you spend in the energy vortex of a particular signpost by thinking about it, the more deeply it is embedded in your subconscious. It's the law of attraction in action: the next time you come across that signpost on the superhighway of life, you'll be far more likely to see a (re)defining moment in the midst of the emotional quagmire. You just need to be going slow enough that you don't miss the off ramp.

• Can you think of any additional signposts beyond the ones suggested? If so, make a list of them and begin to consciously look for them in your daily life. Remember, the practice is to slow down so you don't miss the signs.

CHAPTER 5

The Power of Silence
and Reflection

*Silence Is the Compass That Guides You to
Your Center; Reflection Is the Practice of Recognizing
Your Authentic Self There*

Make peace with silence, and remind yourself that it is in this
space that you'll come to remember your spirit. When you're
able to transcend an aversion to silence, you'll also transcend
many other miseries. And it is in this silence that the remembrance . . . will be activated.

—WAYNE DYER

Are you comfortable with silence? I mean long, sustained
periods of deep silence without any audible sound whatso-
ever. Do you value and seek silence in your life, or do you tend
to avoid it? Before you read on, just sit quietly and ponder what
silence means to you. Take a deep breath and consider how it
feels to *intentionally* sit and "think" about silence in this moment.
Do you ever stop what you are doing and listen to what's going
on around you as well as within you? Right now, is there silence
in your immediate environment or noise swirling around you? Is
that noise outside you, inside your head, or both? The reason I
pose these questions is because it is in the sustained moments of
silence that a vacuum is created in which a (re)defining moment

may be actualized. Oftentimes, it can be well after a (re)defining moment happens when, either by intention or chance, you enter a window of silence and reflection and actually *experience* the impact of that moment. I point this out because silence is the sacred medium through which you fathom the infinite depths of the Original Self. Silence is a sacred continuum that is eternally offering itself to you. You don't have to go on a quest to "find" silence—it's a matter of uncovering it right where you are. Think about it: if all external and internal sounds were eliminated, only silence would remain. It's already there—it's just being covered over by sound. The primary reason more people never actualize their authentic self is because they unconsciously avoid silence, or they are just so focused on what is going on *around* them, on the surface of life, they never create an intentional gap in time and space to notice and reflect upon what is going on *within* them, at their center.

BE STILL AND UN-KNOW

"I am the unknowingness of an unknown mystery.
If you want to know something, go elsewhere.
If you want to un-know everything, then sit and listen.
The silence inside of you is the sound of your knowledge collapsing.
Remember, it is you who said, 'I want to be free.'"

—ADYASHANTI

Many people are not comfortable with prolonged silence—or don't value it—as evident by the amazing amount of noise pollution we, as a culture, create, tolerate, and even perpetuate. To put it bluntly, we are noisemakers; both internally and externally, we are immersed in the noise of our own creation. Beyond the natural and unavoidable sounds nature produces, such as birds chirping, bees buzzing, thunder clapping, rain falling, wind blowing, dogs barking, and so on, every sound we hear is manufactured, in one form or another, by us. Clearly much of the noise we make cannot be avoided because it comes with living in a mechanized society, but consider the noise we make in our heads that perhaps we don't even notice because of all the external noise. Is it possible that we have become so used to, and thus desensitized by, external noise, that in its absence we feel naked, exposed, and vulnerable to the noise in our heads? Perhaps this explains why so many of us choose to immerse ourselves in *additional* external noise whenever we can. Why would we do that? Why would we purposefully avoid the opportunity to be alone with ourselves and reflect upon the silence that is always available if we are willing to seek it out? The easy answer is usually something like, "There's just not enough time in the day to carve out a space for sitting in the silence . . . ," or, "There's no place to go where it is quiet . . . ," or, "What's the use? When I try, my mind just keeps on jabbering . . . ," and so on. The excuses for avoiding silence are legion.

Have you ever been in a conversation with someone who never seemed to take a breath—they just pummeled you with rapid-fire words? Finally, when they do stop talking, you have a new appreciation for the silence it uncovers. (It's times like that when I think a new recovery group called "On-and-On-and-On" might be worthwhile.) What about those who seem to always have the radio or television on, blaring loudly, 24/7, regardless of where they are or what they are doing? When my dog, Mac, and I go for a walk in a beautiful park reserve near our home, it's not at all unusual to pass people on the trails who have their iPod and headphones on, or who are talking on their cell phone, rather than being present in the silence and beauty of nature. Why do people do that? Is it possible they don't create intentional space for silence and reflection because they don't want to be subjected to what it might reveal? If you have a desire to find your way back to your authentic self, entering the silence is not an option—even if, along the way, it reveals obstacles you will need to transcend. The good news, however, is that any obstacles that possibly lie between you and your authentic self are ones *you* made up along the way—and, as you'll soon discover, what you have created, you can also un-create.

Loneliness and Aloneness Are Two Different Things

"Remember: the time you feel lonely is the time you
most need to be by yourself. Life's cruelest irony."
—DOUGLAS COUPLAND

Have you ever had those moments when you felt lonely and cut off from the rest of the world? I have, and I can honestly say those are some of the most depressing feelings one can have. A sense of loneliness can be devastating to your attitude and perspective of life. When you feel truly lonely, your surroundings don't really matter because you are oblivious to the presence of silence *or* noise. You could be physically alone, sitting on top of Mt. Everest without a soul around—or, for that matter, you could be sitting in the middle of New York City's Grand Central Station with thousands of people around—and still feel lonely. Could it be that, in those moments, you most need to be by yourself because something within you is stirring that needs your undivided attention and perhaps has a message for you? If you are mindful, conscious, and willing to be present with your loneliness, you might not only hear what the silence has to say, but you also might discover it's impossible to be truly alone—ever. Perhaps that's the message you need to hear. The practice is to remember that silence is only a breath away, no matter where you are, and to enter it mindfully. What you'll discover is that infinite Presence has never left you alone—It has "let" you alone so you may discover your authentic self. There is a profound difference between loneliness and aloneness. Even in your darkest moments, you are never alone—and that is an empowering truth to remember. Welcome the silence; it beckons you to come closer to who you really are. Remembering you are never alone can, in itself, be a (re)defining moment in the making.

Sharing Silence with Others Connects Us with What Is Real

"You talk when you cease to be at peace with your thoughts."
—Khalil Gibran

Over the years, I have become ever more aware of how important silence is in my life—even in my relationships. Fortunately, my best friend, who also happens to be my wife, Diane, and my second best friend, our dog, Mac, both love silence just as much as I do. This is not to say we don't talk, because we do—a lot. (Yes, that includes Mac, too.) It is not unusual, however, for us to sit together for hours, at home or in the car on long trips, most often holding hands, without speaking at all. It's certainly not because we have nothing to say to one another; it's because there are times when silence doesn't have anything to say to us—it simply invites us to sink below "surface living" and be still. Silence creates an opening that allows us to fully enter into mental "nondoing" where the human self meets the authentic self. We don't have to engage in listening to anything—it's more about disengaging the mind and putting it into neutral, which is when who we truly are reveals itself in all its splendor.

What I have noticed in our relationship is that the quiet moments shared together in stillness seem to create a deeper sense of intimacy between us than, for example, when we are sitting together, being pummeled by noise while watching television or a movie. Perhaps in those moments of silence with infinite Presence, that deepened sense of intimacy between us happens because, *after* those precious moments of prolonged silence, when we do talk, there is no pretense and the conversation is real and laced with authenticity, transparency, gentle loving-kindness, respect, and a sense of gratitude for the life we have been blessed to share. Practicing intentional sacred silence with others connects us with what is real and what most matters—the opportunity for reflection, not only to look into ourselves, but to look into others and see that part of ourselves that gives life meaning and purpose looking right back at us, the authentic self.

Being in Stillness Doesn't Always Mean Being Still

"The stillness in stillness is not the real stillness; only when there is stillness in movement does the universal rhythm manifest."

—BRUCE LEE

Who better than Bruce Lee, one of the world's premier martial artists, to remind us of the importance of stillness when it comes to living in harmony with life? Silence and stillness work in tandem, taking us deeper into the realm of the true Self. Silence opens us to experiencing the absence of noise, but stillness sets the stage. It is how the energy of silence is experienced in real time. Finding the richness of deep silence and stillness in our meditation or quiet time is an important and beautiful experience. However, when we leave that sacred space, although we may have to leave some portion of our silence behind, too often we also leave our stillness behind. We don't have to do that. Although it seems we may not be able to take total silence with us into our daily lives, we can take stillness along because it is a state of mind and, therefore, not subject to outer conditions unless we allow it to be so. By mindfully taking stillness with us into our daily activities, we are also bringing with us a "portable portal" to inner silence. This is another example of merging the deepest part of ourselves, through vertical living, with our horizontal lives, where living on the surface of life takes place. With a conscious embodiment of stillness, we could be riding Space Mountain at Disneyland and still have access to silence despite the external noise all around us. Easier said than done? Maybe so . . . but maybe not. Read on and see.

Bruce Lee's invitation is to mindfully bring stillness with us into the activity of the day. It's not always "easy" to bring stillness along as we enter surface living in a world full of noise, deadlines, traffic jams, business meetings, doctor's appointments, times mowing the lawn, or when changing the baby's diapers. It is simple, however: the practice is to remember to breathe *consciously* and, in the process, recall your mind, to bring it back into your body. Notice that when you pause and take several deep, intentional breaths, you begin to experience a sense of stillness in your interior. Your mind is re-parking itself in your body after having gone for a spin in the far country. You have to breathe anyway, so why not make it a mindfulness practice? Conscious breathing tends to anchor you in your body where the Original Self patiently awaits your return. Something profound happens when you consciously merge your being (the *what*) with your doing (the *who*); stillness fills in the cracks and crevices between your breaths, and you find yourself experiencing your oneness with Life. In other words, regardless of where you are or what you are doing, when you breathe consciously with the intention of anchoring your mind in your body, you are well along on the path to finding your way back to your authentic self, no matter where your body is or what it is doing.

There Is Power in Pausing to Drop the Rock

"The Pause; that impressive silence, that eloquent silence, that geometrically progressive silence which often achieves a desired effect where no combination of words, however so felicitous, could accomplish it."

—MARK TWAIN

Silence plays such an important role in our lives, yet we seldom intentionally pause and anchor ourselves long enough to listen and appreciate the power and potential for the authentic connection silence brings. In my mentoring practice, working with individuals who desire a career in public speaking, I point out the effectiveness of taking an intentional "pregnant" pause every so often, just to allow the listener to catch up and absorb what is being said. Some professional speakers refer to that purposeful pause as "dropping the rock." After saying something you would like to have "sink in," take a deep breath and, as you release the breath, visualize yourself dropping a rock into a deep pond of water, watching it slowly sink to the bottom while at the same time observing the ripples of silence emanating out toward your audience before continuing with what you are saying. The ripple effect of intentional silence can be far reaching when communicating with others. Among other things, it helps create a stronger sense of connectedness or intimacy between speaker and audience—even if your audience is just one person.

Of course, the same can be said for when we are mentally talking to ourselves. The ripple effect of being in silence can be profound if we are willing to pause, enter the silence, and listen to the quiet. If you are like me, there are times when your monkey-mind is on a roll and doesn't want to pause and take a break. If you can be conscious enough to observe your thinking mind zipping along at a breakneck pace, you can choose to stop the mental chatter by intentionally hitting the pause button, taking a deep breath, and "dropping the rock." The deeper the rock sinks, the more calm, serene, and silent the moment at hand will be. As any scuba diver knows, the deeper you go, the more still the water becomes. The same is true for the practice of descending into the depths of inner silence, taking the vertical plunge to the center of our being. The question is, how much silence can you bear? Just consider how many (re)defining moments you may have missed in the past because you made no provisions to pause and intentionally enter the silence of the reflecting pool where the authentic self awaits you in perfect stillness. How deep are you willing to go below surface living to reconnect with who you truly are?

Points to Ponder and Personalize

- Have you become more aware that silence is always available and that it is the perpetual noise coming from either the outside world or within your own mind that covers it? You don't have to go on a quest for silence—you simply need to expose it. Beneath the blanket of all the noise with which you are bombarded on a daily basis lies the perfect silence that serves as a guide to your authentic self. To see how this works in real time, intentionally surround yourself with as much noise as you can possibly bear. Turn on the television, radio, internet videos, people talking, dishes clanging, etc. Then *slowly* strip away one layer of sound after another until you reach silence. Remind yourself that the silence was there all along, and experience the sense of quiet stillness that realization brings to you.

- Can you relate to the example of how often some people continue to talk when they really have nothing to say? Do you fit in that category? Become the observer of your mind, and determine if, when spoken, your words are truly conveying purpose and meaning or are simply filling the empty space. Try catching yourself in action to see if you are creating "noise" with your words. If you are very courageous, you can ask a trusted friend to let you know if, and when, you are talking incessantly, burying yourself in noise. You may discover that you have missed more (re)defining moments than you ever realized.

- Can you discern the difference between silence and still- ness, and do you see the need for both? While silence opens you to experiencing the absence of noise, stillness is a state of mind you bring into your daily life. Remem- ber, mindful breathing is the practice that helps you bring stillness into your day; it is the invisible conduit through which silence makes itself available to you 24/7. As you become more skillful in the practice of mindful breath- ing, you will become far more available to the present moment where your (re)defining moments await you.

- Consider keeping a small rock on your desk, bathroom sink, or any other visible place as a reminder that you can enter the power of silence anytime you so choose. Take time today to, as Mark Twain puts it, experience "The Pause; that impressive silence, that eloquent si- lence, that geometrically progressive silence." You just need to remember to "drop the rock" with a willingness to listen to what the silence *doesn't* have to say.

AS A MINDFULNESS PRACTICE,
CONSIDER THE FOLLOWING:

I invite you to try this and experience the power of silence and reflection:

"To find out what is truly individual in ourselves, profound reflection is needed; and suddenly we realize how uncommonly difficult the discovery of individuality is."

—C. G. Jung

1. Imagine your conscious thinking mind (where the incessant monkey-mind chatter is in full expression) as the surface of a very turbulent ocean. Witness the conversation in which the monkey-mind is engaged. Don't judge it, and don't converse with it—just observe it. By simply acknowledging it from a nonparticipatory perspective, you deplete much of its energy.

2. See yourself holding a beautiful rock, knowing the rock symbolizes your intention to enter silence. Just breathe and be with that intention for a moment.

3. As you take a deep, cleansing breath and drop the rock into the water, notice it slowly sinking down, down, down . . . and out of sight. Then continue breathing consciously and slowly, and notice the sense of calm that arises from the depths of the intentional pause you have taken.

4. Remember that with the breath comes calm, and with calm comes stillness, and with stillness comes the silence within and the opportunity to reflect. It is in the stillness of this silence and reflection that you fully merge with the sacred presence of the true Self; it's also where you'll find the elusive peace you so often miss in the noisy busyness of daily life.

CHAPTER 6

The Practice and Power of Self-Inquiry

Finding, Opening, Asking, and Listening

When you contemplate the nature of the Self, you are medi-
tating. That is why meditation is the highest state. It is the
return to the root of your being, the simple awareness of
being aware. Once you become conscious of the consciousness itself, you attain a totally different state. You are now
aware of who you are. You have become an awakened being.
—MICHAEL A. SINGER, *The Untethered Soul*

In his beautiful book, *Sacred Journey,* Swami Rama recites an
ancient teaching from the *Kathopanishad* that illustrates why
so many of those desiring an authentic life—one that yields a
deeper meaning and purpose—never really find it because they
are looking for it in the wrong place.

An old story is told about the beginning of time. The universe
was in the process of being created, and not everything was
yet in order or fully functioning. Before the universe could be
totally engaged, the Creator had one final task to complete.
To help him complete this task, the Lord summoned an angel.
The angel came. The Creator told the angel that he, the

Lord, had one last job to do in the making of the universe. "I saved the best for last," the Creator told the angel. "I have here the real meaning of human life, the treasure of life, the purpose and goal of all this that I have created. Because this treasure is valuable beyond description," the Creator continued, "I want you to hide it. Hide this treasure so well that human beings will know its value to be immeasurable."

"I will do so, Lord," said the angel. "I will hide the treasure of life on the highest mountain top."

"The treasure will be too easy to find there," said the Creator.

"Then," said the angel, "I will hide the treasure in the great desert wilderness. Surely, the treasure will not be easily found there."

"No, too easy."

"In the vast reaches of the universe?" asked the angel. "That would make a difficult search."

"No," the Creator said, pondering. Then his face showed a flash of inspiration. "I know. I have the place. Hide the treasure of life within the human being. He will look there last and know how precious this treasure is. Yes, hide the treasure there."

While there are other versions of this classic story, this one clearly points to the fact that the greatest treasure of life, the Original Self, has personalized and buried Itself within you as your authentic self—and it lies patiently waiting for you to unearth it so you may draw upon the blessings that come naturally when you are being your true self. As mentioned in previous chapters, it is not a process of "discovering" the authentic self, it's about *remembering* where it is buried. You knew exactly where it was when you were born but, if you are like most of us, the more time you have spent on the planet, the more likely it is that you have forgotten where the true Self has been hiding. If you are earnestly trying to find your way back to the hidden treasure of your authentic self and you are willing to do the work, I have some wonderful news: you don't have to look for, or wait for, your (re)defining moments to pop up along the pathway. You can take a far less circuitous route. Be forewarned, however, it is the road less traveled because it requires commitment and discipline. The other good news is that, once you have become skillful at entering the silence, you are halfway there; the practice is called "self-inquiry."

For thousands of years, masters and students alike have practiced self-inquiry with great dedication because it leads directly to the mother of all questions, which, if you are to ever find your way back to your true North Star—your point of origin—you must eventually ask: "Who am I?" A word of caution, however: it is important not to oversimplify this process because it can be tempting to cut to the chase, intellectually speaking, by thinking you know the answer. In its original context, self-inquiry is very one-pointed; its single purpose is to create an opening through which you, as the seeker, experience yourself "knowing your self" as the Original Self. In other words, it is another version of the *who* (your human self) knowing itself as the *what* (the authentic self) expressing itself as the *who* (your human self). That may sound a bit like mental gymnastics, but in its purest form, self-inquiry is an attempt at dissolving all sense of separation between the human self and the authentic self. In the words of Advaita Vedanta master Ramana Maharshi, "Self-inquiry is the process and the goal also. To hold to it with effort is self-inquiry. When spontaneous and natural it is realization." My sense of what he is saying is, until authentic self-knowing is effortless and spontaneously realized, it is wise to mindfully continue asking ourselves, by means of self-inquiry, "Who am I?" If we don't oversimplify the process, it's quite amazing how many different answers can float to the surface from that one essential question.

To Sincerely Ask "Who Am I?" Is to Begin a Pilgrimage to the Authentic Self

"What question is at the heart of your pilgrimage and your life? What question were you put here to understand?"
—GREGG LEVOY

A pilgrimage is defined as a journey, especially a long one, made to some sacred place as an act of spiritual devotion. As I noted in the first chapter, you may have never thought of the journey of your life as a pilgrimage to the heart of what matters, but, as you'll see, that is exactly what it is. Underneath all the trappings, labels, and circumstances of the human condition—at the center of your being—lies the question you were put here to ask and understand: "Who am I?" That is the question to which we all seek an answer, each in our own unique way.

When I read the above quote from Gregg Levoy's thought-provoking book *Callings*, it stopped me in my tracks and I had to take a deep, intentional breath and process what he was saying. I knew Levoy's words penetrated my soul because I instantly felt that familiar twinge in my solar plexus—the same feeling I get any time I know I am downloading intuitive information and guidance from beyond the level of my intellect. It became clear to me that I was oversimplifying the process. Until that moment, I thought I had done a fairly good job of living in the question "Who am I?" throughout my adult life, but I suddenly realized there was more to know about the process. There are an infinite number of other questions we can and will ask along the way, but "Who am I?" is the quintessential question that underlies them all because the answer defines how we shall integrate with the Original Self. It sets the focus on the lens of our perspective through which we see life. When we fully embody the answer to that question, all other questions will eventually fall away because at the center of who we truly are lies the answer for them all.

After reading Levoy's comment, I sat for the better part of an hour simply marinating in its essence, pondering, "What part of the question 'Who am I?' was I put here to understand that I have not yet realized . . . and has the pilgrimage of my life really taken me closer to knowing the answer?" It was then that I realized that the question "Who am I?" is multidimensional, consisting of many layers that continually go deeper as we do. While the *ultimate* answer may remain the same, it can only be interpreted based on the current level of our consciousness, which automatically skews our perception of the answer. In other words, the process of arriving at the authentic self may require asking the same question countless times throughout our lives and getting various answers based on our current level of evolution as a human being. The key is to keep asking. Essentially, as we deepen in our understanding of the question, the answers will, likewise, continually deepen.

As mentioned earlier, it is vitally important not to oversimplify this process. Intellectually and in theory, who I am and who you are is simple: if the Original Self is all that is and ever has been, then logically, that is who/what we must be. Knowing who we are and *actualizing* who we are, however, are two profoundly different things. Because immediate gratification is rampant in our fast-paced society, it may be tempting to jump to the instant "ultimate" answer rather than to take our time and truly explore what we believe about ourselves. The truth is, whatever our current life looks like is an accurate picture of what we really believe. Self-inquiry is the practice of mindfully navigating the canals of consciousness—what we believe at the deepest level—that take us to our final port of disembarkation, the full realization of the authentic self. Suffice it to say, there are a number of stops on the journey where we may want to linger, falsely assuming we have arrived. The practice is to not mistake the stops along the way as the final destination—and if we are not mindful, that is easy to do. A commitment to conscious and ongoing self-inquiry keeps us moving deeper into the territory where our authentic self was buried when we were born. Self-inquiry helps us remember the way back—it helps us remember who we truly are and, thus, who we were born to be.

Stepping Out of the Shadows and Into Your Own Light

"Often, it's not about becoming a new person, but becoming the person you were meant to be, and already are, but don't know how to be."

—HEATH L. BUCKMASTER

We are all hardwired to seek the freedom to be who we came here to be. When we resist the inherent need to express the authentic self, darkness is created in our lives. When we step out of the shadows of the fear of being judged and into the light of the authentic self, something remarkable happens—we set ourselves free and that new light becomes our beacon, guiding us vertically from the center of our being to the surface of life where we live authentically. To personalize this truth, with my daughter's permission, I share her story. When Merritt was nineteen years old, she sat me down one day and told me she was a lesbian. I was shocked. I had absolutely no idea because she had keep it so well "hidden" for so long. She said she knew from the time she was twelve or thirteen years old but wasn't ready to deal with the consequences of coming out to the world, especially in the conservative community in which we lived. I will admit I did a good job of beating myself up, wondering, had I known, what I might have done different to make it safer for her to embrace who she truly was and live her life openly and passionately, rather than suppressing her authentic self for those precious years.

One day, not long after our discussion, I began reminiscing about her birth and my experience of her as a young child. She freely expressed energy and joy. There was an inherent fearlessness about her, and her soul radiated light—she seemed to twinkle so brightly and effortlessly. She was fully engaged in life. In hindsight, I could see how, in her tween years, it became more difficult for me to recognize that radiance. At the time, I dismissed it due to the uncomfortable divorce her mother and I had recently gone through. Then, the most remarkable thing happened almost immediately after she came out: the radiance of that light became obvious to me again. It was as if that five-year-old child with a passion for everything under the sun had re-awakened within her and unfolded like a beautiful flower for all the world to see. She became not just a new person, but the person she originally was meant to be.

There is no question in my mind that the day Merritt embraced who she truly is was a (re)defining moment for her. It opened a portal through which her true Self arose, she found her authentic voice, and she gave herself permission to be who she really was. That was more than ten years ago. I have to say it was also a (re)defining moment for me because it opened a portal that allowed me to see my beloved daughter through new eyes. It created a deepened awareness of, not only how much I loved her, but also how much I respected her. Today, Merritt and her partner live in Berkley, and she is just finishing a graduate program in integrative medicine and will be specializing in health care for women and children. She also has an intention of having children of her own, which will indeed make me a proud grandpa.

Merritt has a passion and reverence for life because she is spiritually anchored and knows who she truly is. She is one of my greatest heroes because she has shown me what authenticity, self-acceptance, courage, love, commitment, compassion, and transparency look like in action. She made a very conscious choice not to allow herself to be defined by her sexual orientation, and as a result, along with much hard work, she has created an authentic life truly worth living. I believe there is a message there for all of us: it's about giving ourselves permission to step out from the shadows of whatever shrouds the light of our authentic self and love who we are and who we were born to be. And it happens through the practice of self-acceptance.

Peeling the Onion

"When I understand the veil of thinking, what I find is that I am a mystery. I disappear. I disappear as a thought. I disappear as an imagined someone. What I find, if I'm anything at all, is that I'm a point of awareness, recognizing that everything I think about myself isn't really what I am . . . Nobody told us that what we are is a point of awareness, or pure spirit . . . what we were taught was to identify with our name . . . our birth date . . . We were taught to identify with all the memories our mind collects about the past . . . When you stand in your own authority, based in your own direct experience, you meet the ultimate mystery that you are."

—ADYASHANTI, *Falling into Grace*

If we are willing, it can be interesting to witness ourselves exploring the one question that seems to have so many different answers. The process is very much like that of peeling an onion: metaphorically speaking, at the center of the onion is the great "No-Thing" that is the formless Self, the Original Self you truly are, the pure spirit Adyashanti refers to simply as a point of awareness. You have to start where you are, however, peeling from the outside in. It is a process of removing layer upon layer of labels that, until now, may have defined who you think you are. You can begin your self-inquiry with "Who am I?" and from there, continue to peel away the layers. The deeper you delve into the query, the more aware you become that there is yet more to know because every question opens the door to yet another question, and so it goes as long as you are willing to stay engaged in the conversation and keep peeling away the layers. As an example, I'll enter into a brief session of self-inquiry with myself:

The question: *Who am I?*

The answer: I am a man . . .

The question: *Who am I?*

The answer: I am a heterosexual man . . .

The question: Beyond that label, *who am I?*

The answer: I am a father . . .

The question: Beyond that label, *who am I?*

The answer: I am a spouse . . .

The question: Beyond that label, *who am I?*

The answer: I am an author . . .

The question: Beyond that label, *who am I?*

The answer: I am a brother . . .

The question: Beyond that label, *who am I?*

The answer: I am a son . . .

The question: Beyond that label, *who am I?*

The answer: I am a neighbor . . .

The question: Beyond that label, *who am I?*

The answer: I am a Caucasian . . .

The question: Beyond that label, *who am I?*

The answer: I am a North American . . .

The question: Beyond that label, *who am I?*

The answer: I am a victim of a childhood
trauma . . .

The question: Beyond that label, *who am I?*

The answer: I am the owner of a beautiful car . . .

The question: Beyond that label, *who am I?*

The answer: I am a horrible golfer . . .

The question: Beyond that label, *who am I?*

The answer: I am a good musician . . .

Etc.

Can you begin to see the infinite number of layers that cover over the true Self?

At first this may seem like a silly conversation to have with yourself, even if you intellectually know the ultimate answer, but it is a powerful practice if you stay with it long enough. The point is *not* to cut to the chase and immediately say, "I am the authentic self" or "I am the individuated essence of the Original Self." By consciously and *slowly* stripping away the layers, one at a time, you have a chance to witness yourself dis-identifying with so many of the labels that have, to a large part, defined and *confined* your life so far. When fully embodied, the ultimate realization, through the practice of self-inquiry, is that *none of those labels are who you are.* They are the various things you *do* with who you really are. While we'll probe more deeply (and from a different perspective) beneath the labels we wear in subsequent chapters, if you are willing, you can have a very visceral experience with this process by sitting knee-to-knee with someone you trust and allowing them to look deeply into your eyes while continuing to ask, "Tell me who you are" until you have run out of all labels and have reached the simple point of awareness that *what* you truly are is beyond any description. It will take a while, but when you reach the core, you'll know where to find the authentic self that was so well hidden within you long ago.

Using Self-Inquiry to Access Your Compass and Internal Guidance System

"You have to leave the city of your comfort and go into the wilderness of your intuition. What you'll discover will be wonderful. What you'll discover is yourself."

—ALAN ALDA

Once firmly established in the essential question "Who am I?" you can begin to take the practice of self-inquiry into your daily life and use it in a different manner—to draw upon the infinite wisdom that lies within you beyond the finite knowing of the intellect. Some might think of this type of innate wisdom as intuition, and others, as divine guidance. Regardless of what one may call it, it is there to assist in navigating your way on your pilgrimage, not just back to the authentic self but to a life truly worth living. Every day you are faced with numerous decisions to make. You may be faced with deciding between two different job offers, or which of several automobiles you should buy, or if you should accept a date with a particular person, or if you should seek a second opinion on a medical diagnosis, or how to respond to a person who has hurt your feelings . . . and so on. To quote Alan Alda, "You have to leave the city of your comfort and go into the wilderness of your intuition," especially in those times when you may be uncertain about the real questions that need to be asked and their subsequent answers. Accessing your intuitive guidance really does require you to enter the "wilderness" of that quiet place within you where no one else can follow. Your intuition is the very still voice arising from the authentic self. When you are confronted by a circumstance that requires a choice or decision, this modified version and practice of self-inquiry can make the journey not only easier, but far more rewarding. Rather than asking, "Who am I?" the practice is to follow this seven-step process:

1. Determine the question for which you seek guidance.
2. Create the space, take time to enter the silence, and find your breath.
3. Open your heart, and ask your question.
4. Listen with no agenda, letting go of what you think *or* hope the answer will *or* should be. (This intention removes the ego and keeps it from tainting the process.)
5. When an answer comes, embrace it and sit with it. Don't debate with it. You may or you may not like the answer, but in either case, don't cling to it or push it away—just be with it.
6. Breathe deeply, noting that the answer may give birth to a deeper question to be asked. If it does, and if you are willing to stay engaged in the dialogue, ask the question that is revealed. (If no other question arises, you have your answer. Just be sure it's not the egoic-self camouflaging the response.)
7. Go back to step 4 and follow the same process until your heart informs you that you have arrived at an authentic resolution to the original question. You'll know when you have arrived because there will be a deep sense of peace that accompanies the final answer. That is because you have drawn on the wisdom of the authentic self.

The Practice Is High
Involvement and Low Attachment

". . . for any one of us to have an authentic deepening . . . we must let go of truths that we currently hold [cling to], make space in consciousness for the revelation of something more, something deeper, wider, higher, and perhaps even less tangible. This requires great faith. Indeed, to be asked to give up that which we have securely sequestered away in our mind as the only truth, as the only way it can be, is scary."

—FROM *The Art of Being: 101 Ways*
to Practice Purpose in Your Life

What I have discovered is that the fourth step in this process is where things get real. Having an open mind as you move forward is an essential and powerful way to evolve. The practice is to dive into self-inquiry with a high level of involvement in the process and a low attachment to the idea that we have nothing more to know, do, or be. As long as we live, there will be deeper truths to explore because we are surrounded by infinite possibilities. Are you willing to enter into a conversation with yourself, knowing that beneath the original question there is another underlying question awaiting you, and then yet another one still? The good news is, just like on the hit game show *Jeopardy!*, the ultimate answer is already right in front of you—you simply have to keep asking the right question to get to it. Be mindful in asking that question because the universe conspires to help you discover the answer in ever-evolving ways so you can then move on to asking from yet an even deeper place of knowing. The bottom line is, the deeper you go into "Who am I?" the more you grow, and the more you grow, the more you'll know there is yet more to know.

Points to Ponder and Personalize

- Can you relate to the ancient story regarding where the Original Self personalized and hid Itself in you? Have you ever caught yourself looking for the meaning and purpose of your life everywhere but within yourself?

- Have you noticed how easy it is to avoid the process of self-inquiry? H. W. Shaw wrote, "It is not only the most difficult thing to know oneself, but the most inconvenient one, too." Commitment to the journey of self-inquiry is what separates the dreamers from the doers. The key to an effective and long-term shift in your beliefs is to not oversimplify the process of self-inquiry by intellectualizing the answer. It takes time to shift your consciousness. It took years for you to assimilate all the various labels you currently wear that so easily cover the authentic self; it is unwise to think you can peel them all off in an instant. If need be, seek the assistance of a supportive person and experiment with the "knee-to-knee, eye-to-eye, tell me who you are" process. It is a powerful way to kick-start the practice of self-inquiry.

- Can you see yourself using the modified seven-step self-inquiry process as a way to access your intuitive guidance system? The next time you find yourself pondering a decision that needs to be made in your linear life, remember the seven-step process. You may be surprised by the clarity that is revealed. Remember, your intuition is the voice of the authentic self making itself available to you 24/7. The question is, are you taking time to open, ask, and listen?

- A pilgrimage is a journey, especially a long one, made to some sacred place. There is nothing more sacred than the journey to the authentic self. Can you see yourself on a pilgrimage, a sacred sojourn of the soul, returning to the source from where it came? Self-inquiry is the sequential process that sets the stage for a (re)defining moment because every moment of every day opens the portal to the infinitely deep well of the Original Self. It provides the opportunity to live consciously, moving forward, knowing there is more to know about who you really are.

CHAPTER 7

Rocking the Boat

Whose Life Are You Living?

Why join the navy if you can be a pirate?
—STEVE JOBS

It's one thing to feel that you are on the right path,
but it's another to think that yours is the only path.
—PAULO COELHO

I have a rhetorical question for you. Please read it as if you had never thought about it before because, in so doing, you may be priming the pump for a true (re)defining moment:

> *Have you ever had others criticize you for the path
> in life you have been called to walk, be it spiritual,
> career, lifestyle, education, relationships, and so on?*

The reason this is a rhetorical question is because we know we all have faced the opposition of those who are firmly convinced that what we're doing is all wrong. Just by slowing down and taking a deeper look at this question, we begin to see how often we brush this issue aside and, in a manner of speaking, deny that it is an issue at all because it may be too painful to contend with the pushback and consequences. The curious thing is that when we really stop and consider it, quite often, those who tend to have the greatest opposition to the path we walk are those who we think would be most supportive: family and friends. It can be challenging to stand toe-to-toe with those we love and care about and tell them that their path is not ours. Many of us live in denial of who we truly are because we fear losing someone or something—and there are times that if we don't rock the boat, too often the one we lose is ourselves. We lose our sense of self, our dignity, our faith, our sense of purpose, our joy, and, most important, we lose our way back to the authentic self we came here to be.

Of course, the aforementioned question can be extended to include religious institutions, political parties, and cultural traditionalists—many of whom are well ensconced in the belief that their way is the *only* way. It can be incredibly difficult to separate ourselves from the vortex of the collective consciousness and go our own way because the gravitational pull of the common voice is so strong. Yet if we don't follow our true path, we know there is a part of us that will slowly begin to die. Call it Spirit, Soul, Life Force, or what you like, there is that within us which knows who it is we've come here to be and what it is we've come here to do. If we don't listen to and honor its call, it begins to wane. This is when life becomes more about enduring until we die rather than thriving while we are here.

Who Is Sailing Your Ship?

"Never had I understood that I command, with absolute authority, the ship of my life! I decide its mission and rules and

discipline, at my word waits every tool and sail, every can-
non, the strength of every soul on board. I'm master of a team
of passionate skills to sail me through hell's own jaws the
second I nod the direction to steer."

—RICHARD BACH

As you probably know by now, I am a fan of metaphors with a
message that make life a more meaningful experience. I resonate
with the above quote by Richard Bach because it is a brilliant
metaphor reminding us that we give the sailing orders and set
the compass for our ship of life. It is a wake-up call to the fact that
we are the masters of our own destiny through the development
and use of the skills of conscious intention, commitment, self-
discipline, accountability, and passion—all of which are needed
to get us to the destination of an authentic life truly worth living.

If this metaphor works for you, it makes good sense that the
captain of your vessel must be your conscious, decision-making
mind, and the wind that drives the vessel forward is the impar-
tial energy of the universal law of cause and effect that effortlessly takes the vessel in whatever direction and depth the captain
(that's you) sets the rudder of intention. It's very easy to be lured
into complacency, allowing any number of people or things—
including family, friends, the economy, the media, and so on—
to become the influencing factor that sets the direction in which
our lives will be led. That's why it's important to remember, as
Bach infers, you can choose to command, with absolute authority, the ship of your life, each and every day, one day at a time . . .
one (re)defining moment at a time. Perhaps that is a mantra
worth writing on a piece of bright yellow sticky paper and past-
ing it on the bathroom mirror, the refrigerator, or the dashboard
of the car as a reminder to repeat it a few hundred times every

morning before we set sail into the new day: "I command, with absolute authority, the ship of my life!"

So understanding that your vessel follows the direction of your "nod" (agreement) and that the precious cargo your vessel transports is the essence of your wisdom-collecting soul self, what kind of sailing orders will you issue to the crew (your conscious intention, commitment, self-discipline, accountability, and passion) when you get out of bed and set sail tomorrow morning? Be mindful of what you agree to because the Universe conspires to make it so. Your crew is ready, willing, and able, and they await your command. Give some thought to who is sailing your ship; you'll enjoy the journey on the surface of your life so much more when your authentic self is at the helm.

The Difference Between Trying to Fit in and Knowing You Belong

> "Fitting in is about assessing a situation and becoming who you need to be to be accepted. Belonging, on the other hand, doesn't require us to change who we are; it requires us to be who we are."
>
> —BRENÉ BROWN

Imagine a large jigsaw puzzle that, when completed, depicts the image of the life you have always wanted. Then notice that the puzzle is nearly complete and the only piece missing is you. In order for you to fit into the only open space in the puzzle, however, you have to reshape yourself to conform to that space formed by all the other puzzle pieces. The message is, if you don't "fit in," you don't belong in the picture. How does that visualization make you feel? Most likely not too happy, and perhaps even resentful. This, however, is exactly what many of us do. We shape ourselves to the specifications others have established before we are accepted and allowed to be part of the picture. I know from whence I speak because I spent the first half of my life continually reshaping myself to fit into other people's puzzles. I really didn't know who I was and their picture of life looked pretty good to me—and let's face it, when we don't know who we truly are, any picture is better than no picture, or so we think. It feels good to be accepted, loved, and approved of by others, but often the membership fee to belong to that club is far too high of a price to pay.

Know When, Why, and How to Separate Yourself from the Herd

"The individual has always had to struggle to keep from being overwhelmed by the tribe. If you try it, you will be lonely often, and sometimes frightened. But no price is too high to pay for the privilege of owning yourself."
—FRIEDRICH NIETZSCHE

It is very comforting knowing you belong. The problem is that too often we confuse belonging *in* the tribe (knowing we are one with it) with belonging *to* the tribe. One offers the freedom to be who we are while in the presence of those we love and care about; the other offers restriction and a limited sense of self-definition based on the opinions of others required to fit in. You'll know when you belong *in* rather than *to* your tribe because you will feel a sense of freedom and expansion—a compelling call to be your authentic self and who you really are, to express your unique individuality with no conditions attached. Part of truly belonging is knowing that you are encouraged to bring the unique gift of your whole self in such a manner that the innate wholeness of the group expands because of you; you are consciously enriching others by your presence and the gifts you choose to bring, rather than by conforming to their needs. When you are free to be yourself, the essence of that "something" larger than you naturally spills over into everything you say and do, bringing with it the affirmative life force of your authentic self.

The challenge, as Nietzsche infers, lies in not allowing ourselves to be absorbed in the collective consciousness of the tribe to a point where we lose our individuality; when that happens, we also lose our way back to the authentic self. It is in this context only that, what Nietzsche calls the "tribe," I refer to as the herd. Animals travel in herds, schools, flocks, pods, prides, and packs—it's only natural we would as well. It feels wonderful to hang out with other human beings. Plus, there can be great safety and comfort in numbers—and that's a good thing. The work, however, lies in remembering we are not animals but soul-based individuals and not allowing our individuality to get trampled by others. The irony is that those who choose to keep their "specified" place in the formation of the herd *to* which they belong are *unique*—just like everybody else—they simply may not know it because running with the herd creates so much dust, no one can really see how unique they truly are.

Forgive the cowboy talk, but I trust you get the point. I don't use the word *herd* with any disrespect but, rather, as a metaphor that describes a way of limited thinking that implies there is safety in numbers and as long as one is willing to travel in the direction the herd is going, life will be easier and less risky. In reality, that may be true, but at what cost to your soul? When traveling with the herd, are you finding your way back to who *you* authentically are, and were born to be, or to someone else's idea of who you are or should be? Nietzsche was spot-on when he said that the privilege of "owning yourself" comes at a high price, but you are worth it, right? Remember, at times it may get you in hot water with those who seek to usurp your individuality out of their own fear-driven need to keep the status quo, but knowing how and when to cut from the herd is not a novel idea. Many rebels have demonstrated how to set themselves free from the herd.

> "Jesus promised His disciples three things: that they would be entirely fearless, absurdly happy, and that they would get themselves into trouble."
>
> —W. RUSSELL MALTBY

When you fearlessly follow the truth that calls to you, getting into trouble is almost certain. Regardless of the path you walk, you will always encounter those who feel threatened by your authenticity. Being absurdly happy isn't the only benefit of following the path *you* were born to walk; it will, as the teacher said, "set you free" and at the same time, encourage others to transcend their own limited vision of themselves. The result, of course, is the peace that passes all understanding, along with a bunch of mavericks blazing their own unique trail back to the authentic self they each are.

Have You Made an Agreement
with Life to Stay Small?

"To discover your core self, you must be willing to break the agreements you have made with mediocrity. The moment you stop running the racket of staying small to please society, family, friends, or bosses, your original face will start to come into focus and you will know who and what you really are as an emanation of the universal one."

—MICHAEL BERNARD BECKWITH

Perhaps what our critics don't understand is that beneath the layer of what they may refer to as a "choice" to follow a different path, there lies another layer where the authentic self lives and from where its voice perpetually whispers ever so softly in our inner ear, "Be who you authentically are and you'll find freedom, fullness of expression, joy, peace, purpose, and meaning in this precious life you have been given." This voice beckons us to—as my friend Michael Beckwith infers—break the agreements we have made with mediocrity by staying small to please others. The mystical thing is, when we hear and *listen* to that voice, it's not so much that we are then guided to "choose" a certain path in life but, in truth, realize and accept that our path has chosen us. Do not, however, consider this a "get out of jail free" card for the less-than-great choices we all have made along the way that may have caused pain and suffering in our lives or the lives of others. The reality that our path chooses us when we are ready in no way alleviates the fact that we are always personally accountable for the choices we make in our day-to-day lives. The voice to which I refer is incapable of guiding us in a direction that is self-destructive or harmful to others or in any way dishonors the sacredness of life.

If you don't follow your own unique path, at the end of the day, when you draw your very last breath, you will ask yourself whose life was it you did live. It is never too late to begin living your own life, being the true Self you are. You just have to remember that, at times, you may have to separate yourself from the herd. The practice is to remember, as Nietzsche put it, there is a difference between belonging *to* the tribe (like a possession) and losing yourself in it, as opposed to belonging *in* the tribe and being one *with* it, knowing you are free to roam wherever your path takes you without fear of being banished from the tribe. Don't think for a moment that making a conscious choice to separate yourself from the herd, if and when it is appropriate, is not a (re)defining moment in the making, because that is *exactly* what it is.

Do You Stand Behind What You Say You Believe?

"We are so constituted that we believe the most incredible things; and, once they are engraved upon the memory, woe to him who would endeavor to erase them."
—JOHANN WOLFGANG VON GOETHE

Goethe was correct—it can be risky business to challenge someone to examine their beliefs. We need look no further than to Socrates, who was put to death because he was teaching young people to challenge authority, "think" for themselves, and derive their own beliefs from within. We could say some of the local tribesmen didn't particularly like him trying to separate the herd. Do you ever take time to sit and deeply think about the beliefs you hold as true? Occasionally, it is a good thing to do, to just review what you hold as sacrosanct and then consider the source from which those beliefs came. It could be a belief related to your spiritual or religious views, political views, worldviews, cultural views, racial views, or any of the other legion of topics that occupy your life. The question is, whose beliefs are they that you call your own—and when and how did you develop those beliefs?

As an example: with all the unrest in the world, and especially within our own political system, now is the perfect time to consider the source from which we drew the political ideals and values we might hold so dear. This is not at all to imply that what we believe isn't the truth (for ourselves); it's simply an invitation to consider how we came to accept it as our truth. Most of us inherited our beliefs and core values from our parents, and that can be a good thing—or, in some cases, perhaps not such a good thing. The same could be said about our teachers, bosses, ministers, and others who played an influential role in our early years. The real question is, do we *really* believe what we say we believe? Sometimes we don't really know what we deeply believe until we take time to consciously explore those beliefs and see where they live within us. As mentioned in the previous chapter, self-inquiry is a practice we can and should do on a regular basis. This is especially true if we catch ourselves avoiding self-inquiry because of the discomfort it might stir up.

One telltale sign of how deeply we are rooted in our beliefs (or not) can be found in our need to force them on other people. I respect those who are so on fire with their beliefs that they want to "share" them with the world—however, insisting that I should accept their beliefs as my own just because they passionately believe them is an entirely different thing. This is a perfect example of how, too often, we lethargically allow others to have free rent in our heads and we mindlessly take on their beliefs as our own because we have not invested the time and energy to consider what it is we really do believe. After all, it is much easier and less painful to let others tell us what we should believe. I wonder how many of us sit there and watch the ads on television for certain pharmaceutical products, political candidates, ballot issues, and so on, and just take it all in as gospel rather than personally researching the issues before we embrace them as truth. Just because it is on television or the internet doesn't mean it is true.

The same could be said about our religious indoctrination. Just because someone who wears sacramental garments or has a title in front of their name said it doesn't necessarily mean it's true. The truth lives within us, not on television, on the internet, or anywhere else. Discerning what is true for each of us is an inside job, where we leave "surface thinking" behind and take the vertical path to our own center and listen. This is where the real inner work comes in: to challenge our own beliefs is not always easy because they are often tied with invisible guilt strings to those who gifted us with their beliefs. Examining and challenging what we believe, however, is one of the greatest things we can do as we mature—it allows us to clarify and deepen the beliefs and convictions that honor who we are today and wish to become in the future . . . and in the process, discard the beliefs that no longer work for us.

Challenging your own beliefs can serve as a filtering system that enables you to compare what is in your mind with what

is in your heart and to confirm there is a congruency between
thought, feeling, and belief.

If you are willing to mindfully challenge what you think and say what you believe, you may find that what is rattling around in your head and so easily tumbles out of your mouth doesn't honor what you know lies deeply embedded in your heart. If that's the case, with a little mindfulness, you can choose to release those old beliefs and entertain a new notion about what is true for you today. The most empowering thing is, you don't have to get permission from others to do so. What you'll discover when you reach this point of self-acceptance is that the more deeply you hold a personal belief, the less compelled you'll feel to debate it with others. This does not mean you can't or shouldn't share what you believe with those who ask; it simply means you will feel free to explain your perspective, but you will not be compelled to argue or defend why you believe differently from others. A lack of desire to debate or defend your beliefs does not mean you have no passion for what you believe—it simply means you have taken time to examine your beliefs and have found great peace in them. Surrendering the need to fit in is very liberating; it will set you free to be who you truly are. Do you really believe what you say you believe? Just think about it and be open to following where it takes you . . . perhaps even to the portal of your next (re)defining moment. Goethe and Socrates would both be proud of you.

POINTS TO PONDER AND PERSONALIZE

- Would you say you belong *in* your tribe or *to* your tribe? It's easy enough to discern—one leads to freedom of authentic expression and the other leads to repression. It takes courage to march to the beat of your own drum because it separates you from the herd and potentially makes you a moving target for your critics. Can you see the relevancy of this theme in your life today? If so, the practice is to remember that when you honor the authentic self you came here to be, although you may stand out, it's also what shapes your character and makes you uniquely you.

- Take a deep breath and sit with the question, "Whose life am I living today?" What is the first image that rises in your field of awareness when considering this question? Is your path one you were "called" to by your own passion, or one you took to please someone else? This is a vital question because many people have been living someone else's life since the day they were born. Awareness is always the first step to initiating any type of change, especially one that puts you on the vertical path back to your authentic self.

- Are you free to have a difference of opinion with others and express it without fear? Can you say "no" to others, and at the same time, do you offer them the freedom to say "no" to you? Once you become more fully grounded in living from your authentic self, if you are led to decline someone's request, you won't have to justify your position. You'll simply convey, in either words or actions, that in rejecting their request, you are not rejecting them. Learning when it's appropriate to say no to others—and having the faith and courage to do so—is liberating.

- Do you find the idea of carving your own unique trail back to your authentic self intimidating because you believe you may have to go it alone? The practice is to remember that, if it's authentically *your* path, as unique as it is, you do *not* walk that path alone. You may not visually see them, but countless millions of other people are walking their own unique paths, and the ever-present Infinite Intelligence that put you here is your—and their—constant traveling companion.

CHAPTER 8

The Hero's Journey

The Bliss You Seek Is Seeking You

The self is not a known territory, but is a wilderness. Too often we forget that. Too often we reach the boundaries of what we know about ourselves and turn back.

—PAUL FERRINI

I am continually on the lookout for real-time examples that offer positive evidence that living authentically is possible—*and* that the (re)defining moments that get you to that way of life are constantly popping up in front you. The only caveat is that you have to be able to recognize them and step through the portals that open because they don't stay open long. In the context of this chapter, those who linger miss the boat to their bliss. Three of the things that will most quickly hurl you through that portal when it opens are passion, purpose, and courage. When you live your life passionately, purposefully, and courageously, wherever the path may take you, happiness naturally follows you like a shadow on a perpetually sunny day—and the good news is, when you combine passion, purpose, and courage with happiness, bliss soon follows. You'll discover that your bliss *will find you* when you are authentically being who you were born to be *and* doing what you came here to do. Metaphorically speaking, the bliss you seek is seeking you, but it loves to play hide-and-seek, and at the moment, you are "it." Your bliss has hidden itself very well within you . . . and I'll give you a hint where to find it: consider looking between the cracks and crevices of your heart's deepest desires and your greatest *natural* talents.

You can't make or fake bliss because it flows naturally and directly from the authentic self; ours is to follow its lead. However, here is the challenge: while we may daydream about following its lead and perhaps even take a few steps on the path back to the authentic self, too often the tendency is to come to the edge of our comfort zone, the known, and then turn around and retreat because you have reached unexplored territory and there seems to be so much at stake to lose. This chapter is about igniting your passion for life by understanding that your highest purpose can only be realized through consciously aligning with your authentic self and then courageously harnessing the power it gives you to step through the portals created by your (re)defining moments when they open. And they will indeed open *if* you are willing to go beyond the safety of the known and happily follow the path where your bliss takes you.

The Hero's Journey Is One of Honoring the Call of Your Authentic Self

"Follow your bliss . . . if you do follow your bliss you put yourself on a kind of track that has been there all the while, waiting for you, and the life that you ought to be living is the

one you are living. When you can see that, you begin to meet
people who are in your field of bliss, and they open doors to
you. I say, follow your bliss and don't be afraid, and doors will
open where you didn't know they were going to be."

—JOSEPH CAMPBELL

In the 1970s, when I first heard the phrase "Follow your bliss,"
popularized by mythologist Joseph Campbell, it immediately
hooked my attention. While studying the ancient wisdom teachings of the Upanishads in a college philosophy class, I heard the
word *bliss* used frequently but never really stopped to consider
what it meant in practical terms. My dictionary defines the word
bliss as "Extreme happiness, ecstasy, and serene joy." As a marketing major at the time, I can tell you that this sort of bliss was
not even on my radar.

One day on campus, after a heated debate in that philosophy
class about the "wisdom" of following one's bliss, I had an
epiphany that altered the course of my entire life. It started out
as a conversation with myself and evolved into a chain of
thought-provoking ponderings about the possible consequences
of Campbell's admonition. Was he saying I could follow a career
path that would make me extremely happy . . . one that brings
joy and a smile to my face . . . and that doors would open effortlessly for me, providing me with the means to live well? But
what would my parents think? I became a marketing major because my dad was my hero and made a great living as a vice
president in a major ad agency. It was then I realized I was following my dad's path rather than my own. Why? Because, not
only did I want to honor him (and make the kind of money he
was making), I wanted to *be* him. The realization I had was that,
in the process, I was really dishonoring myself. I wasn't aware of
it then, but what was about to happen "in" me throughout the

next few days as a result of the realizations that came to me that day would be among the most memorable in a lifelong series of "ah-ha" (re)defining moments.

This was the day I set out on the path that Campbell refers to as the "hero's journey," and I must admit, it was a bit more than scary at the time. I felt very little like a hero knowing (fearing) I had to tell my dad something that could easily provoke the dragon out of his cave. Please note, this is the scenario and conjecture I drew in my own head and had nothing to do with him because, as it turned out, he was overjoyed I was making a conscious choice to challenge the path I was on. It seemed he knew all about the "follow your bliss" thing and had gone through his own version of it long before he heard the term. Who knew? It's quite amazing how often we create our own dragons of limitation based on the assumptions we project on others. That is the hidden power of the fear of disapproval hard at work.

> "The way to find out about your happiness is to keep your mind on those moments when you feel most happy, when you really are happy . . . deeply happy . . . Stay with it, no matter what people tell you. This is what I call 'following your bliss.'"
>
> —JOSEPH CAMPBELL

That day on campus, my epiphany was setting the stage for a (re)defining moment because I knew in my heart I would never be happy studying economics and market trends or selling someone else's ideas and products. Taking Campbell's guidance seriously, I began to focus on what I was doing in those moments when I was most happy, and I noticed something very important: those very same moments were also when my passion and joy were flowing freely and my natural talent was being expressed. Just a few days later, a new door opened for me—a (re)defining moment was about to happen, and it was huge. As it would turn out, my bliss would be found on an entirely different path than marketing. Between classes, while sitting on the grass, playing guitar, and singing with friends I had made on campus, it became obvious where I would find my happiness—it was right there in front of me: for three years, I had been hanging out with people who had nothing to do with the business school. These folks were following their bliss—as music majors. No wonder I was always with them in my free time. They were modeling the life that was calling to me—I just wasn't ready to see it. When I was ready, it forced me to finally pay attention to that still, quiet voice within me I had been ignoring (or at least avoiding—or more likely, denying) for a very long time. Do you remember the "nudges" we feel within when the creative urge to be more fully and authentically expressed begins to stretch and push out? I had ignored those nudges until they became pushes, and finally shoves, and my friends served as the perfect mirrors I needed to help me look into myself and see that I was not honoring who I was born to be.

> *This is where understanding your reason for being on the planet comes in and how important it is to honor that purpose. In the self-inquiry process, the natural question to follow "Who am I?" is "Why am I? . . . What is my purpose for being here?"*

When we are young, we seldom think about our purpose and why we are here, but even then, when we are in the proper growing environment and willing to give ourselves permission to fully own our discontent, we are far more likely to feel and explore the nudge when it pokes us. Although admittedly, the question "Why am I (here)?" really wasn't one that was bouncing around in my head all that much in those days, there was, nonetheless, something that caused me to feel that nudge and follow it down the rabbit hole, not knowing where it would take me . . . and that is a deep hole. "Why am I?" is a profound, multifaceted question explored from many angles throughout this book. Ultimately, the fast-track answer is, you are an individuated vessel in which, through which, and *as* which, the Original Self expresses in an infinite number of unique ways. The operative words here are *expresses* and *unique*. It's important to remember that it is only through integrating fully with your authentic self that your uniqueness and how you express it are revealed. Your authentic self is continually trying to get your attention so it may be more fully expressed. The lesson to be learned here is that when your (re)defining moments pop up, be prepared to go where you had no plans on going—because that is where your bliss awaits you.

In short, after three years of college as a marketing major, I changed my major to music and never looked back. I had found my bliss. That day, sitting on the grass with my friends, was a true (re)defining moment for me because I was able to recognize the door to a deeper part of myself as it swung open. I am quite sure that was because I was willing to embrace my discontent on the path I had been walking as a marketing major—and *at the same time*, I was able to feel and follow that divine nudge to deviate my course. As one door closed, another door had opened, and in the process, I began to understand what Joseph Campbell meant when he said "follow your bliss." This also marked the beginning of a whole new relationship with a word I had, many years prior, locked away in the recesses of my mind as neither practical nor safe: *trust*. What I have learned since then is that *trust* is not just a word; it is an action taken based on a deep knowing that you are part of something far greater than yourself that, when actualized, knows how to guide you to the authentic life you have come here to live and so richly deserve.

Following Your Bliss Offers Countless Serendipitous (Re)Defining Moments Along the Way

> "Seek out that particular . . . attribute which makes you feel most deeply and vitally alive, along with which comes the inner voice which says, 'This is the real me,' and when you have found that attitude, follow it."
>
> —WILLIAM JAMES

Did music turn out to be a lifelong career path? It did for about ten of the happiest years of my life and then, one day, while performing for a group at a spiritual conference in Monterey, California, another door appeared before me labeled, "Now, follow your bliss through this door." That was the day I met my future mentor, Dr. Frank Richelieu. As you may recall from chapter 4, I had "happened" upon Dr. Frank by no mistake via television a year earlier. Through my affiliation with him and the Centers for Spiritual Living, I stepped through a portal that put me on a new pathway of self-discovery by studying the metaphysical teachings of Ernest Holmes. I followed that path, which ultimately became a fulfilling career of public speaking and teaching spirituality for the next quarter century. In 2008, however, my soul began to stir again, telling me there was something more for me to do. It was then, as if by some mystical, serendipitous occurrence, another door appeared before me and flung itself wide open. One day, through a chance e-mail exchange, I met Joel Fotinos, who ultimately became my publisher and a wonderful friend. I submitted a book I had originally self-published, and Tarcher/Penguin picked it up and republished it. That book is *The Art of Being: 101 Ways to Practice Purpose in Your Life*. Its success led to a second book, *The Art of Uncertainty: How to Live in the Mystery of Life and Love It*. Both became award-winning books and, as a result, the book you are reading was born. Yet another is in the birth canal right now—all because, forty years ago, a mythologist named Joseph Campbell put a wild notion in my head that if I would only be willing to follow my bliss, the Universe would sequentially open the doors that would take me to a life I never dreamed of and sustain me each step of the way—one step, one door, one (re)defining moment at a time. I can gratefully say the Universe has kept Its part of the bargain ever since.

I share this story with you not because it is all that special but because it illustrates the point that *anyone* who is willing to leave the well-trodden path and embark on the road less traveled can do the same thing. Is it easy to follow your bliss? Of course not—that is why Campbell calls it the "hero's journey." To complete the hero's journey, you must depart the safety of the castle (the known), venture out into the world (the unknown), confront whatever stands between you and your purpose for being, and return a changed person. You'll have a chance to encounter every dragon (fear) that lives within the darkest caverns of your mind that wants to keep your life small and safe— I can attest to that. (Re)defining moments don't happen just one time in your life; they happen every time you make a decision to follow your bliss, again, and again, and again. New doors are awaiting your arrival; the big question, as Joseph Campbell puts it, is whether you are going to be able to say a hearty "yes" to your adventure.

Your Talent Is Waiting for You to Set It Free So It Can Set You Free

"Use those talents you have. You will make it. You will give joy to the world. Take this tip from nature: The woods would be a very silent place if no birds sang except those who sang best."

—Bernard Meltzer

Recently I watched a television program in which comedian and actor Jim Carrey was being interviewed. The program was a retrospective of his career, sharing insights on his journey from his young-adult years to his present-day life. If you have followed his career, you would probably agree that he has never been one to shy away from expressing his natural talents in "unique" and creative ways. Carrey could be the poster child for demonstrating the courage it requires to "put yourself out there" and offer your gift to the world without attachment whether others like it or not.

What I found most fascinating was his attitude about change and his willingness to follow his passion for creative expression through many unknown twists and turns. As Erica Jong wrote, "Everyone has talent. What's rare is the courage to follow it to the dark places where it leads." By "dark places," I believe she was not referring only to the unexplored shadow side of the egoic-self, but also the authentic self within that lies silently in the shadows of our own ignorance that is there, and always has been, patiently awaiting our arrival through the vertical passageway of our (re)defining moments. In other words, when we allow the talent gifted to us by the Creator to emerge from within the core of the authentic self, it takes on a life of its own and guides us where we need to go to honor its expression. The hook is, we have to be passionate and courageous enough to follow that talent, especially into the dark places where it may appear we are all alone, always remembering that is an impossibility because the authentic self is right there the entire time. Jim Carrey seems to have mastered the willingness to follow his talent where it wants to go, and the result speaks volumes about who Carrey knows himself to really be.

With humility and a very large grin on his face, Carrey described the many so-called coincidences that happened at the most unexpected times, involving people and events that moved him forward on a career path that appeared to have a mind of its own. While he didn't use the phrase "(re)defining moments," in my opinion, that is exactly what they were because each change he went through allowed (or forced) him to dig deeper and find a new piece of his creative self he had no idea was there. He cited the many changes he went through in the process of his own evolution, starting as an impressionist, then moving on to be a standup comic, then becoming a television actor, and finally becoming a movie star. In his early years, when he was working as an impressionist, he had no idea he would one day be one of the most recognizable faces in show business; he just kept stepping through the doors as they opened with a willingness to see where they would take him. It would be safe to say he was following his bliss.

If there is one thing Carrey is, he is authentic. Love him or hate him, he leaned into the recesses of his own mind and heart and pulled out his own authentic, unique brand of humor that, few will dispute, is distinctively his—and because of that, he has continuously and courageously (re)defined himself and his career a number of times by going where he had not been before. At moments during the interview, when looking back at his journey, he seemed genuinely surprised by his own success—a success that came because it he was unabashedly committed to following his passion through unexpected doors as they opened, trusting that his unbridled desire to bring joy to people and make them laugh knew where it was going. At the end of the interview, the host congratulated Carrey on his fine body of work and the success he had enjoyed and then asked him to share what his next project is. Carrey's face lit up instantly and, excitedly, he replied, "It is going to be *the* best, most creative, innovational, and successful thing I have ever done." The host said, "Wow! That is great! What is it?" With that wide, toothy, "cat that ate the canary" smile on his face that has become his trademark, Carrey replied, "I have absolutely *no* idea."

Are You an Innovator or an Emulator?

"All life is an experiment.
The more experiments you make the better."
—Ralph Waldo Emerson

Are you an innovator or an emulator? Your willingness to experiment with your life determines the answer. If there is one thing all individuals who are innovators have in common it is that they are more inclined than most people to naturally seek and follow their bliss. We are all hardwired to do the same, but innovators are more likely to own their originality and, therefore, willing to blaze their own unique trail rather than follow the well-trodden paths of others. Regardless of the field of interest in which they are drawn to play, they are, by nature, curious and willing to experiment with the life they have been given. Note that when I say they "experiment with their life," I don't mean they are putting their physical life in danger but, rather, they use the life they have as a "learning laboratory" that allows them to explore the creative process, putting new, unique, and untried ideas to the test. This mind-set is a natural gateway to the authentic self.

True innovators probably have few, if any, (re)defining moments because, whether they know it or not, they are *already* working from the deeper place of the authentic self where every moment is seamlessly stitched to the next. Again, are you an innovator or an emulator? One points the way, and the other waits for the way to be pointed. True innovators know who they are, and they passionately and courageously hang their authenticity out there, openly flapping in the breeze, without attachment to what others think about them or their ideas. On the other hand, emulators wait around for the innovators to set the bar and then, when it is safe, they do their best to be like them, to emulate them. Which of the two do you think is more likely to be on the hero's journey? Perhaps the better question is, which of the two do you think is following *their* bliss?

Are You Listening to Your Bliss Meter?

When we think of innovators, people such as the Wright brothers, Thomas Edison, Henry Ford, Susan B. Anthony, Marie Curie, Bill Gates, Steve Jobs, Steven Spielberg, Oprah Winfrey, and countless others may come to mind. Yet the person sitting next to you in a restaurant might also deserve a spot on that list. Or it might be the person you see staring back at you in the mirror. Innovators are people just like you and me who are willing to experiment with the life they have been given rather than keeping it neatly tucked in a box of conformity because it is safer to hang out in the center of the herd. They are willing to fully live from the authentic self, even if they don't consciously know that is what they are doing. Is there a risk in experimenting with your life? Of course there is. But if you put your ear to your bliss meter—your heart—you'll hear your soul tapping out an SOS saying, "Let . . . me . . . out." How you respond to that SOS determines if you are an innovator or an emulator—or perhaps more accurately stated, whether you are blazing your own unique path or simply following the trail of others because it seems less risky or less work. Your true bliss will never be found by imitating others. Experimenting with the life you have been given automatically places you on the path to countless encounters with your authentic self, but you have to take the first step in faith, even when there is no tangible proof to support you.

We don't always have to wait for our (re)defining moments to show us the way to our bliss. Sometimes just by experimenting with life outside our box we'll stumble right into our bliss.

My dictionary defines the word *experiment* as "a course of action tentatively adopted without being sure of the eventual outcome." Right out of the gate, this definition implies that life is risky. Emerson is spot-on when he says all of life is an experiment. That *is* life—one big, bodacious experiment. The reality is we have been experimenting and risking since the day we were born. That is how we learned how to walk and talk—one contiguous process of trial and error, making mistakes and learning from them, discovering what worked and what didn't. However, as we age, life appears to get more risky and we develop a greater sense of attachment to the status quo because we fear we have more to lose. In the process, we tend to get more set in our ways, experiment less with the life we've been given, and sit by while our dreams become smaller and smaller. As a result, the life force within becomes a little less vital because its inherent nature to push out, to grow, to expand, is not being honored. Any time we experiment with anything, we take a risk of making a mistake, and perhaps that's where the real fear lies. No one wants to make a mistake when it comes to experimenting with their life—perhaps that's because they confuse *making* a mistake with *being* a mistake.

> "Too often, we choose to settle for the status quo because of the risk involved with new discoveries. We fear we may make a 'mistake' venturing outside our box (current reality) and so we settle in for the long run, living our lives with an inner knowing that there is something greater awaiting us beyond our comfort zone. It woos us, inviting us to move forward into the unknown where anything is possible, including making mistakes . . . so we hold back. The belief is that

mistakes are a bad thing. The fact is that a person who has
never made a mistake has never tried anything new. Yes, it
is safer not to make any mistakes, but that means we have
to live small, restricted, redundant, and unrewarding lives,
which is not what you and I were sent here to do. We have
been sent here to grow and evolve consciously, to expand our
horizons. A fear of making mistakes drastically limits those
horizons, doesn't it? Well, it's easy to stop making mistakes:
Just stop having ideas, stop growing, stop living."

—FROM *The Art of Being: 101 Ways
to Practice Purpose in Your Life*

The key is to not personalize your mistakes, thinking they reflect who you are, because they don't. Many people define
themselves—or allow others to define them—by their mistakes,
and it doesn't have to be that way. The practice is to observe
yourself and your behavior and witness where you are resisting
experimenting with your life because your identity is so wrapped
up in how the world perceives or defines you. Prove to yourself
that making mistakes is not necessarily a bad thing. Start small,
perhaps by going to a restaurant that serves a type of food you
have never tried. Adopt the mind-set that if you don't care for
the food served, going to that restaurant was not a mistake; it
was an experiment that proved positive because you learned
from it—you *grew* from that experiment. Then expand your experiment to include a sampling of music, theater, sports, and so
on—anything that is new to you. Then, consider enrolling in a
class that takes you into new territory for your mind and maybe
even your body to explore. No experiment is a mistake if your
consciousness embraces it as a learning experience. As I have
mentioned throughout this book, remember that any moment

can become a (re)defining moment because contained within it is the opportunity to see your life through entirely new eyes and be changed by what you see. Experiment with your life—you may discover a whole new dimension of who you are. In the process, don't be surprised to see your bliss following right behind you like your shadow.

POINTS TO PONDER AND PERSONALIZE

- Can you relate to Joseph Campbell's explanation of bliss? How do your mind and heart meet with the idea that there is a direct correlation between authentically being who you are and the degree of bliss (happiness, ecstasy, and joy) you experience in your daily life? Do you think it is really possible to follow your bliss, or does it seem more like wishful thinking? Be careful how you answer these questions because the Universe is listening.

- If you are not already on the hero's journey, what would it require for you to embark on this path? Remember, you can't make or fake your bliss because it arises naturally from your conscious connection with the authentic self. If willing, a good place to begin the hero's journey is with a bit of self-inquiry. Begin by asking yourself these questions:

  1. On the pathway I currently walk, is my soul being fed and am I expanding my sense of being who I really came here to be?

2. Are happiness, ecstasy, and joy a part of my daily life and, if not, am I willing to do what it takes to create them? In other words, am I merely surviving, traveling on the surface of life until I leave this planet, or am I thriving, moving forward, knowing that happiness and bliss follow me as I honor my unique purpose for being here?

3. Do I trust that there is an inherent Intelligence in me that knows how to guide me on my hero's journey . . . and am I willing to follow Its lead, knowing I will likely encounter every dragon (fear) that lives within the darkest caverns of my mind that wants to keep my life small and safe?

4. Knowing they point the way to my bliss, am I using the inherent natural talents the Creator imbued in me—and if not, why?

5. Do I consider myself to be an emulator or a true innovator—one who is able to carve my own path back to the authentic self, a path I know no one else can blaze for me?

6. Am I willing to see my life as a "learning laboratory"? Do I give myself permission to make mistakes and not beat myself up for having made them, seeing them as growth opportunities that move me toward the authentic life I have come here to live?

• The point of asking yourself these questions is that they are the catalyst for action you must take prior to undertaking the sojourn of the hero's journey. You must be willing to draw upon your God-given talents, remembering that is the deep well from which your bliss will arise—and then trust the process, knowing the right talents will appear at the right time, opening one door after another in perfect time and space if you are able and willing to do your part. If you are like most people, you may have more than one talent, so how will you know which ones you were meant to use? Remember, there is a profound difference between what you "like" to do and what you were "born" to do. This will be more fully explored in the final chapter.

- You'll find purpose, passion, and most important, the courage to follow your greatest gifts at the core of your soul, where your bliss meter—your heart—is patiently tapping out that SOS: "Let . . . me . . . out . . ." The practice is to remember that even in those times when it may appear you are most alone on the hero's journey, the authentic self is right there, loving you and guiding you every step of the way. Clearly, choosing to heed the call of that SOS is a (re)defining moment because you are honoring and aligning with the source from which the call is coming—your authentic self.

✳

CHAPTER 9

The Seven Intrinsic Qualities of the Authentic Self

How to Know When You Have Arrived

The end of all our exploring will be to arrive where we started and know the place for the first time.

—T. S. ELIOT

There is a profound wisdom to be found in Eliot's above statement. As I have mentioned throughout this book, our real journey is one that takes us back to our point of origin, who we were the moment we were born, before the world began shaping us like dolls with a wardrobe of various masks covering over the authentic self. This presents a bit of a conundrum because if, upon our remembrance, we are to know the authentic self as if for the first time, how shall we recognize it? How will we know what authenticity looks and feels like through all the disguises and masks we have grown so comfortable wearing? The irony is most of us have spent years—decades upon decades—unknowingly putting greater and greater distance between our human self and our authentic self, not so much in physical terms but in mental and emotional terms. And yes, it has everything to do with the egoic-self who thinks its job is to keep us as far from the authentic self as possible. Why? Because the closer we get to the authentic self, the less power the egoic-self knows it has over us. The egoic-self is very resourceful in creating a false illusion of separation from the Original Self by crafting some very convincing masks that shroud the authentic self—which, remember, is that point within where the Original Self has left Its unique imprint. (Note: Don't confuse these disguises with the labels we wear discussed in chapter 6, such as *smart, dumb, short, tall, fat, skinny, capable,* or *incapable,* which pertain to one's personality, appearance, character, and behavior.) When worn long enough, in our forgetfulness, we begin to assume these masks represent who we are and, therefore, they end up defining us. The egoic-self is a master mask maker, and we wear its many disguises—most often, unaware that we are doing so, not having a clue there is really much more to who we are. Make no mistake about it, a (re)defining moment occurs the moment we make a conscious choice to peek at what lies beneath these masks. That action takes us below "surface living" on a vertical path leading directly to our center, where the truth of who we really are lies in smiling repose.

> "Every man is a divinity in disguise, a god playing the fool."
> —Ralph Waldo Emerson

As I have mentioned, I love when life gives me exactly the perfect metaphor to illustrate a point I want to make. As I write this chapter, Halloween is nearing, and the holiday always brings back memories of many years ago when my wife, Diane, and I picked up our two grandchildren, Cailin and James, to go trick-

or-treating. James, who was eight years old at the time, was wearing a terrifying rubber mask of the grim reaper, while Cailin, who was six, wore no mask at all; she was going as the kindly "Good Wizard." When I asked her why she wasn't wearing a mask, she very matter-of-factly replied, "Grandpa, Good Wizards can't wear a mask because then nobody would know they were good." Of course, this is our story and our journey—to remember the authentic goodness we are, even beneath our many masks.

> "Where's your will to be weird? . . . The most important kind of freedom is to be what you really are. You trade in your reality for a role. You give up your ability to feel, and in exchange, put on a mask."
>
> —Jim Morrison

In this chapter, we take an unabashed look at the many layers of masks and false beliefs the egoic-self holds in place in a manner that covers over the goodness of who we really are. Unveiling the authentic self is not only a process of peeking under the many erroneous masks the egoic-self projects, but also knowing what we are looking for. The real question is, as we peel off the many masks, how will we know when we finally arrive where we started, knowing that place, the authentic self, as if for the first time? The answer is simple. When *consciously* living in the presence of the authentic self, seven intrinsic qualities will naturally rise in the field of our awareness, and they can't be missed or ignored. I encourage you to intentionally take your time in moving through this chapter because the result of doing so will not only open your eyes to who it is you have truly come here to be but also help you understand why it has been so difficult to locate your authentic self up to this point. Don't be surprised if you see the same mask showing up in more than one of the seven intrinsic qualities. As you are reading this chapter, make an effort to witness how, even now, the egoic-self will try to divert your attention; it will do *anything* to keep its many masks in place. This chapter is lined with potential (re)defining moments if you have eyes to see and ears to hear them popping up—first in your heart and then in your mind. The practice is to listen with your heart and then process what is revealed with your mind. So let us begin.

The Seven Intrinsic Qualities of the Authentic Self

1. WHOLENESS

> "Wholeness is not a condition; it is a state of being."
> —DR. FLETCHER HARDING

While it has been said the Whole is greater than the sum of Its parts, the truth remains that without every part, the Whole would not be complete. The authentic self knows it is an individuated aspect of the Whole because It remembers from where it came—it knows it is a vital part of the Whole, a microcosm of the Macrocosm. An awareness of this truth creates balance and an understanding that wholeness is inherently ours now because it is not a condition we arrive at one day; it is a state of being—nothing can be taken from or added to the Wholeness of the Original Self—the All that is.

One of the first telltale signs that we are living from the authentic self comes in those unmistakable moments when we feel a

sense of effortless connection with everyone and everything—
with the Whole. This is when it gets real and all things artificial
fall away, leaving only a sense of oneness with life in the moment. This is when we discover that true wholeness is a state of
being, not a condition or a point at which we one day arrive
when all things are perfect, because that will never be the case
in the human experience. Wholeness is a place in consciousness
that affirms we are one with life, intuitively knowing that
below "surface living" is all *already* perfect, just the way it is—
and just the way we are. When we live fully anchored in the
awareness of our unity with the Whole, authenticity is revealed.
Something real emerges from within us, and all sense of separation dissolves. When that happens, notice a (re)defining moment opening before you; notice how the feeling of wholeness
floats to the surface of your life, even in the face of circumstances, conditions, and events that may normally contradict the
typical notion of wholeness. Nothing is missing in that moment
because you have transcended the egoic-self that relies on the
material world for its identity.

This awareness alone will begin to remove a few of the
masks the ego has been holding in place for so long, such as
shame, which comes from a mistaken belief that we are somehow flawed and, therefore, not enough; or the mask of lack,
which comes from a mistaken belief there is not enough of
whatever we need to feel complete; or the mask of the perfectionist, which comes from the mistaken belief that when we can
finally control everything and everyone else's opinion of us and
garner their approval, then and only then, we'll be complete. To
live in the awareness and presence of the authentic self to is remember we are whole and, therefore, complete, just the way we
are, warts, wrinkles, and all.

2. REVERENCE

> "Above the cloud with its shadow is the star with its light.
> Above all things reverence thyself."
>
> —PYTHAGORAS

> Because of its connectedness to the Whole, the authentic self
> knows that all people and living things are an extension of
> itself. When we live consciously in the presence of the au-
> thentic self, reverence naturally arises and we are guided to
> know that to do harm to another would be to harm one's
> self. Reverence gives birth to compassion and acts of loving-
> kindness, which manifest as harmony, peace, and joy.

Having reverence for any person or living thing is recognizing
the presence of Life within the form and honoring it as sacred.
When living from the authentic self, practicing reverence with
others is not a difficult thing to do because we remember we are
connected with that person or thing at a very fundamental level
and we come from the same essence, the source of all that is—
the Original Self. Reverence awakens us to a deep understanding that to do harm to another is to do harm to ourselves. As we
make that connection, realizing that all living things are one
with the great Whole, we are naturally led to treat each person
or thing as we would desire to be treated—with nonjudgment,
loving-kindness, and compassion. I have heard it said that, instead of flowers, Dr. Ernest Holmes would often dine with a
vase of weeds from his garden on his dining room table. He
considered it a beautiful reminder that the creative intelligence
of the One flows equally through every living thing and that the
only difference between a weed and a rose is the value (judgment) we choose to place upon it.

A few of the masks that conceal the intrinsic quality of reverence found when living from the authentic self are the mask of the judge, worn by one who labels everything and everyone based on external appearances only; the mask of selfishness, worn by one who mindlessly takes from others and life in general, using everyone and everything, including the earth's resources, with no thought of giving back to life; the mask of the terminator, who is so disconnected from their feelings (soul) they have no regard for life in any form and, thus, they never concern themselves with how their words and actions affect others; or the mask of the unconscious one, who, failing to realize they walk a sacred earth, leaves a thoughtless trail of discarded "stuff" for others to clean up. Of course there are many others, but suffice it to say, it requires great courage and mindfulness to remove these masks and face life with reverence. Consciously living in the presence of the authentic self sets the stage for a (re)defining moment because it invokes reverence and compassion, which then flows naturally into everything we say, think, and do, making all of life a sacred experience. That is, literally, a beautiful thing.

3. Fearlessness

"Fear not what is not real, never was and never will be.
What is real always was and cannot be destroyed."
—Bhagavad Gita (400 b.c.)

Because the authentic self is one with infinite Life, it knows only the present moment; to the authentic self, the past and the future do not exist. All fear we experience is attached to a concern about loss of some sort, which may or may not take place in the future, be it five seconds or five years from now. The concern of loss may be real or imagined; fear is often founded on remembered experiences from the past which then get "re-imaged" and projected into the future. Fear is an energy that has no life of its own, other than the one we give it. To live from the authentic self is to allow its fearlessness to keep us anchored in the present moment, which is our only true point of power.

To say that fearlessness is an intrinsic quality of the authentic self does not deny that fear can be a real experience in the human condition, and that is exactly the point—it is a *human* experience, not an experience of the true Self. The authentic self has no concept of fear because it has no concept of loss, only the wholeness of Being in the present moment—and Being is not subject to anything in the human condition.

Fear is probably the most universally worn mask because our attachment to loss has so many tentacles. A short list of our fears might include the loss of our loved one's life or our own, our health, a relationship, financial status, reputation, job, physical strength, beauty—most of us especially fear the loss of control of "what is" in the moment—and so on goes the list. The masks behind which our fears linger are legion, such as anger or rage, which is the fear of losing control over something or someone else's behavior or actions; jealousy, which is the fear of losing someone's affections; envy, which is the loss of self-esteem by fearing that you are not enough; worry, which is the fear of a loss of any or all the aforementioned in your future; and _____ (fill in the blank, describing your most predominant fear). If any of these masks fit, ask yourself what is holding them in place. If you examine it closely, you will discover it has something to do with your mind being in some space in time other than *this* sacred moment, which is the only time a (re)defining moment can occur. The practice is to be here, now, and see if you can open to the presence of the authentic self that is always with you, knowing its fearlessness is yours. Remember to breathe.

4. INTEGRITY

"Integrity simply means not violating one's own identity."
—ERICH FROMM

Being fearless, the authentic self, when actualized, can only speak and act from the "integrated" nature of its oneness with the Whole, and integrity naturally manifests outwardly as honesty and pure intention. When consciously "integrating" our awareness of the presence of the authentic self, our thoughts and actions are clear and are in alignment with our integrity. We communicate what needs to be said to others and ourselves with honesty, compassion, and transparency, even when the truth may be difficult to speak or hear. Because it is so fully integrated in its unity with the universal Whole, the authentic self is incapable of violating itself. It knows only integrity, even when no one is watching.

Once an old and very wise master teacher took his students into the village late one night, saying to them, "I am old and helpless and have no money. Go and follow people who are walking alone along the dark side streets, and when no one will see you, pull them into a dark corner and take their money. Do them no harm, but bring me the money." All the students readily agreed but one, who replied, "But master, there is never a time when no one will see me because my Self is always observing what I do." With this, the master shouted with joy, saying, "Alas, there is one among you who knows the truth about who he truly is! Let this be a lesson by which you all live your entire lives."

While I am uncertain of the origin of this ancient story, the moral it conveys and affirms is that the intrinsic quality of integrity is available to us when we align with the authentic self. There is a distinct difference between integrity and honesty and how they work as a team. Think of honesty as a verb—it's the action of how we conduct ourselves on the surface of life when we are anchored in an awareness of the authentic self that dwells at the center of our being. The word *integrity* comes from the word *integrate* (from the Latin *integratus*), which means "to bring together all parts into the whole." Integrity is the inner knowing of the truth about ourselves and allowing it to sublimate through our mind and heart from the core of our being; it's the melding or "integrating" of the awareness of the authentic self within, into our every breath, every thought, and every action, wherever we are and in whatever we are doing. Integrity, then, is the *inner* knowing and remembrance of our unity with the whole, and honesty is the *outer* action—how we demonstrate it in the world. In real time, we can consider the intrinsic quality of integrity and the action of honesty as one, because when embodied, they wrap themselves around each other and become as one common thread, which is then finely woven into the fabric of our lives.

Some of the masks that hide the authentic self and, thus, the intrinsic quality of integrity, may appear on the surface to be very innocuous. It doesn't have to be blatant or criminal acts of dishonesty, or even acts of betrayal or infidelity, because most people are very cognizant about those issues. Sometimes it is the "everyday" subtle issues that sneak under the radar when living close to the surface of life: it could be the mask of "unconscious lack" that says nothing about the mistake the cashier made by giving us too much change back. Perhaps it's the mask of the "pleaser" who recoils at the thought of telling someone what we really think because it might evoke an undesired or feared response—or telling them something we don't, in our heart of hearts, truly believe, simply to gain favor with them. When we live from the authentic self, the intrinsic quality of integrity moves through us in a way that gives us the strength and courage to be the person we know we came here to be—even when no one else is watching. These are moments that define who we are from the deepest point within and, by no coincidence, bring with them the peace that passes all understanding, not because we seek it, but because it seeks us when we intentionally live with integrity from the inside out.

5. HUMILITY

"Do you wish to rise? Begin by descending. You plan a tower that will pierce the clouds? Lay first the foundation of humility."

—SAINT AUGUSTINE

"If you want to reach a state of bliss, then go beyond your ego. Make a decision to relinquish the need to control, the need to be approved, and the need to judge. Those are the

three things the ego is doing all the time. It's very important
to be aware of them every time they come up."
—DEEPAK CHOPRA

Humility is a complex word because it can mean different things
to different people. Humility is traditionally defined as "the act
of being modest and respectful." It is also a synonym for *humble-
ness*. In addition, in many metaphysical, contemplative, and spiritual traditions, humility is seen as a virtue—deliberate actions
motivated by other than the egoic-self. It is in the context of this
definition that the authentic self exists as humility. Being anchored in wholeness and fearless honesty, the authentic self has
no relationship with the egoic-self and, therefore, has no need to
be validated, approved, loved, or feared by others. Living from
the authentic self does not mean we don't honor other people's
opinions, but we are not attached to them. Humility creates
space for others to have an opinion of us and the world, be it
positive or negative, without making them right or wrong—
primarily because we know who we truly are.

Generally, when we think of the antithesis of humility, we
come up with descriptions such as *egotistical, braggadocios, prideful,
opinionated, self-important, superior, arrogant, conceited, vain,* and so
on, and these descriptions may all be correct when we consider
them as disguises or masks that conceal the authentic self. The
collective energy hidden behind all these masks, however, is fear
and the need for love and approval. It seems that people who
seek the most approval tend to feel the most powerless, while
those who seek the least approval often feel the most powerful.
That is because people who seek the least approval tend to know
who they really are and, therefore, from where their true power

comes—the authentic self. (Note: In this description, I am not referring to those who operate arrogantly with a false sense of confidence that comes from the egoic-self.)

In his groundbreaking book *The Seat of the Soul*, Gary Zukav tells us we are all on a quest for power; the question is, are we turning within (vertically to our center) to find it, or to the world (horizontally, on the surface of life)? If we turn within, toward the soul-self, what we'll find there is what he coined "authentic power"; if we turn to the world, our quest leads us to pursue what he coined "external power." The primary difference between authentic power and external power is that one is internally and eternally available to us while the other is always temporal, subject to coming and going, depending on outer current conditions. Similarly, in his classic book *The Seven Spiritual Laws of Success*, Deepak Chopra refers to the inner quest as "Self referral," meaning to look within to the true Self rather than without for our power and identity. Conversely, Chopra refers to the external quest as "object referral."

These are perfect examples that point out the difference between living life horizontally, on the surface, or vertically, from the center of our being. Both Zukav and Chopra are pointing us in the right direction, *if we have ears to hear and eyes to see*. When we feel powerless, the tendency is to seek power in the form of external things (objects) such as money, position, physical strength, beauty, sexuality, possessions, job titles, and so on—all of which fuel the egoic-self's ongoing quest for external power because it knows it has no power of its own. If we are not mindful, it is quite easy to allow these external items to define us.

When we feel weak and powerless, the temptation is to slip on masks that allow us to become whoever we think we need to be to garner power from the world and in the eyes of those whom we believe represent our power. In the process, we conceal the intrinsic quality of the authentic self, known as humility, as it lies in silent repose awaiting our recognition of its presence. Many disguises conceal the intrinsic quality of humility, such as the masks of the macho, the winner, the intellectually superior (or inferior), the rich one, the strong one, the victim, the bully, the beauty queen, and the perfectionist. If you look closely behind these masks, you'll see they are all tied to a need for love and approval because, somehow, we still haven't learned we are enough—and that were born "enough."

Humility is a natural state of being when we live from the awareness of our oneness with Source. We know we don't have to manipulate or coddle anyone or anything because we are directly connected to our power within. When living with an authentic sense of humility, we define ourselves and our world gently and nonjudgmentally because we place ourselves neither above nor below any other person. The view of a life worth living is quite beautiful from there.

6. EQUANIMITY

> "And what You are is the great Unborn, timeless and eternal, in its [1]st-person perspective as the great I—I, the great Self, the Witness of this page, and this room, and this universe, and everything in it, witnessing it ALL with a passionate equanimity that leaves you alone as the Unmoved Mover."
>
> —KEN WILBER

Equanimity is a balanced and even state of mind with the soul. It means being anchored in a state of mindfulness that is never disturbed when our human emotions (either negative or affirmative), pain, or other circumstances rise to the surface of life that may cause other people to lose their balance. Equanimity is an intrinsic quality of the authentic self because, as an individuation of the Original Self, it has no opinions—it is incapable of judging—it is the Silent Witness of "what is" and is unattached to what it sees because it exists outside the realm of the material world and the human condition.

When living from the authentic self and aligning with the intrinsic quality of equanimity, we are less likely to be moved by opinions, appearances, or conditions because the true Self never favors *or* disfavors what is in the moment. It observes and feeds that information back to us at a human level in a manner that puts us at choice. It allows us to either respond or react— and there is a big difference between the two, depending on the state of balance between our mind and soul in the moment. It may help to think of equanimity as evenness of mind, which transcends the egoic-self because it is neither pumped up nor depressed by what is. This in no way means that to live with equanimity is being cold, hardhearted, or uncaring—it means we are perceiving whatever is in the moment through the neutral eyes of the Silent Witness. Just as the morning sun shines on all beings equally because it is incapable of judging some of us more worthy of sunlight than others, the same is true of the authentic self. It is incapable of judging good or bad; it finds neither favor nor disfavor with what is happening in the moment. Equanimity allows us to become the discerning observer of life and practice mindfulness of being in a manner that fully integrates the remembrance of wholeness as a state of being that is available to us at our center, not a condition on the surface of life at which we will one day arrive when all is perfect.

The masks that can conceal the authentic self and, therefore, the intrinsic quality of equanimity, are many. The primary disguise, which is one of the egoic-self's favorite masks, is judgment. Let's be clear that there is a huge chasm between judgment and discernment. True discernment aligns quite well with the authentic self because discernment is an observation of "what is" with no opinion and no emotion attached to it. Judgment, on the other hand, is laced with opinions and fueled by strong emotions. Most of us will admit that, when unchecked, our minds do a marvelous job of dashing out in front of us and slapping labels of "good," "bad," "right," "wrong," "preferable," "not preferable," "wonderful," "tragic," "beautiful," "ugly," "fortunate," "unfortunate," and so on, on just about everyone and everything. If you stop and really look underneath those words, you'll find strong emotions and opinions driving them. Living from our authentic self avails us of the intrinsic quality of equanimity that allows us to step back from our emotions long enough to breathe and see a deeper truth beyond all appearances and conditions, regardless of what they are. In times when "what is" in the moment can pull us out of balance, equanimity is a gift from the Original Self that brings us back, making that moment a portal for a (re)defining moment if we are mindful enough to see it and step through it.

7. LOVE

"Love is the self-givingness of the Spirit through the desire of Life to express Itself in terms of creation . . . Love is free from condemnation, even as it is free from fear. Love is a cosmic force whose sweep is irresistible."

—ERNEST HOLMES

The authentic self is the direct descendant of unconditional love. When we strip away the many masks we wear, at the core of who we really are, we shall find the essence of love in its purest state. It is unconditioned because it is without form—love was, and is, the initiating spark of all life—the alpha and the omega and everything in between those two points. It permeates, animates, and sustains all living things, holding itself back from none, judging no one or no thing. The authentic self is love because it is the microcosm of the great Macrocosm, the Original Self, Infinite Intelligence, Being, Presence—call It what you choose. In its highest vibration, unconditional love is the glue that holds all that is together and exists beyond all "conditions." Most important, love has selflessly individuated and imbued itself within us at that point we call the authentic self.

Since antiquity, masters, poets, writers, songsmiths, and just about every other human being has sought to fathom the eternal depths and the meaning of love, including from whence it comes and why some people seem to experience it more than others. The ancient Greeks fully understood the complexities of this issue. They believed that one word could not adequately describe such a powerful and all-encompassing energy, so they divided love into four categories: *eros,* meaning romantic love; *storge,* meaning love for family; *phillia,* meaning love for friends and neighbors; and *agape,* meaning unconditional love of, and for, the divine. Agape love has been defined as unconditional love because it is absolutely indiscriminate in the giving of itself. In his book *Awareness,* the mystical Jesuit priest Anthony de Mello describes the indiscriminate nature of unconditional love so eloquently and in such practical terms, it's hard to miss the point: "Is it possible for the rose to say, 'I will give my fragrance to the good people who smell me, but I will withhold it from the bad'? Or is it possible for the lamp to say, 'I will give my light to the good people in this room, but I will withhold it from the evil people'? Or can a tree say, 'I'll give my shade to the good people who rest under me, but I will withhold it from the bad'? These are images of what love is about." Can you sense the indiscriminate nature in which life bestows the gift of itself with no strings attached? Can you see yourself as a recipient of this magnitude of love? Because regardless of whether you know it or not, you are.

Metaphorically, consider the idea that we are each filters through which love flows without condition and that it is we who, at the level of our consciousness, our belief system, shape and direct how love manifests in our lives. Perhaps this is why the Greeks had different names for love, because it can show up differently at different times. Understanding that the authentic self is the direct descendant of unconditional love means that love *already* lives within us in an unconditioned, formless state, until we give it form by how we shape it with our thoughts and intentions. This leads us to the obvious question, if the source of this love is absolutely indiscriminate, holding back from none, why do we, who are recipients of and vessels for this love, discriminate and hold back our love from certain others? We hold back because we tend to identify with the egoic-self, which is busy keeping score, trying to separate those who are unworthy of our love from those who are worthy—as if there were only so much love to go around.

What disguises might your egoic-self be holding in place that shroud the authentic self and, therefore, conceal the gift of unconditional love? Judgment is, without question, the mother of all masks, and nothing separates us from authentic love more quickly than it does. In fact, judgment seems to be a "normal" part of the human experience. Judgment has many compelling disguises that we don't think of; the masks of jealousy, envy, resentment, rage, anger, insecurity, gossip, inferiority, superiority, and intolerance are just a few of the variations on a theme called judgment. It's important to remember that judgment, in all of its disguises, is really fear. It's equally important to remember that fear dissolves into the nothingness from which it came when exposed to the light of authentic love and an awareness of the oneness from which we have all come. Think about it: if the authentic self is the direct descendant of unconditional love, that makes you the perfect delivery system for it on this planet. All that is required is a willingness to bring your being into your daily doing. In other words, love is a noun you have the opportunity to turn into a verb. That is what (re)defining moments are all about.

You'll Know When You Have Arrived

At the beginning of this chapter, I posed the question, how will we know when we have arrived at the authentic self and know it as if for the first time. The answer lies in building a conscious awareness of these seven intrinsic qualities and then mindfully keeping them in the forefront of our mind and daily activities, knowing that, in doing so, we are automatically called to higher ground. When the qualities of *wholeness, reverence, fearlessness, integrity, humility, equanimity,* and *love* become the norm in our daily lives rather than the exception, we'll know we are living from the authentic self. With mindfulness, we'll be able to catch ourselves wearing any number of disguises that, until now, have unknowingly defined us and kept us separate from the authentic self. It is only then that we can challenge the beliefs that have kept the masks we've been wearing for so long in place. This is why our (re)defining moments are so important; each one brings us closer to the being we know we truly are beneath the many masks. Perhaps my granddaughter, Cailin, really did say it the most succinctly on that Halloween night so many years ago: when we remember the goodness of the authentic self that inherently lies beneath our many masks, we'll no longer feel compelled to put on a disguise and pretend we are someone other than who we really are. That awareness is the sweetest treat ever.

Points to Ponder and Personalize

- Were you able to discern a few of the masks you may have been wearing without even realizing what you were doing? If so, can you "own them" without judging or beating yourself up? The first thing needed in any conscious evolution is an awareness and acceptance of "what is"—even if it isn't what you might like it to be. It is only then that you can do something about it. This awareness alone opens the portal of a (re)defining moment called "What can be."

- Finding your way back to the true Self is not an overnight journey, but it is reachable by taking small steps, one day at a time. It's about changing your consciousness by slowly implanting new ideas and desires in your mind.

I've spoken previously about "top-of-mind" awareness utilized in product marketing to build an unconscious awareness about a product—the more often someone sees something (even if in the moment they don't desire it), the more likely they are to automatically buy it when they do desire it. To personalize this strategy, think of top-of-mind awareness as a way of training your mind to regularly focus on what you want, rather than what you don't want. The practice is to daily embed the seven intrinsic qualities of the authentic self deeply into your consciousness. In so doing, you'll be far more likely to access those qualities when you catch yourself slipping on a mask that conceals who you really are. To reinforce this habit, try the following as a "training tool."

PRINT THE SEVEN INTRINSIC QUALITIES OF THE AUTHENTIC SELF, EACH ON A SEPARATE PIECE OF PAPER, AS AN AFFIRMATION

- *I Am Wholeness*
- *I Am Reverence*
- *I Am Fearlessness*
- *I Am Integrity*
- *I Am Humility*
- *I Am Equanimity*
- *I Am Love*

When finished, place them at different points in your home where you'll "see them" even when you may not realize you are seeing them. A few great locations include your bathroom mirror, your refrigerator door, your computer screen (or screen saver), the dashboard of your car, a wall in your office, the inside of your front door, and the headboard of your bed. Keep in mind this isn't a process of creating something that is not already there—it's simply reminding you where to look. This is a process of subtraction, not addition; it's about removing old beliefs that no longer serve you and allowing yourself to see and celebrate the wholeness of who you really are. This is also how you'll know you have arrived where you first started and know it as if for the first time. There will be little doubt in your mind that you have just met face-to-face with a (re)defining moment.

As a Mindfulness Practice, Consider the Following:

You will need a pen and paper because this may take a bit of time. But finding your way back to your authentic self is worth the effort, isn't it?

1. Go back and take another look at the masks identified in this chapter. Be aware this is an exercise about you, not the others in your life who may well have their own masks. Sit in silence with each mask for several minutes and see if it fits; if it does, write its name on the paper. While you may

be able to easily identify some masks you wear, some will be less obvious, so notice any temptation to deny what your heart may tell you is a mask you have been wearing without even realizing it.

2. After you have your list, review each mask, one at a time. Ask yourself if you can see how wearing that mask has somehow served your egoic-self's agenda to keep you feeling separated, powerless, and apart from the peace, authentic power, and freedom that comes when living from your authentic self.

3. Once you have identified the masks you wear, you have the choice to keep them on or remove them. If you choose to remove them, I caution you to not try to pull off the masks because to do so often makes them cling more firmly. By mindfully and faithfully choosing to focus on the seven intrinsic qualities that lie on the other side of the masks and making a sincere effort to actualize those qualities, you'll notice that, over time, the masks represented begin to slowly fade away and are replaced by the authentic you.

CHAPTER 10

The Seamless Self Emerges

Finding Your Authentic Voice

No one man can, for any considerable time, wear one face to
himself, and another to the multitude, without finally getting
bewildered as to which is the true one.
—NATHANIEL HAWTHORNE

When I think of the authentic self, I am reminded of a
credit card commercial that was popular years ago. The
hook was, "MasterCard—don't leave home without it." Likewise, we could say, "Your authentic self—don't leave home without it." The truth is, you can't leave home without it because the
authentic self is an inherent part of you and goes where you go.
Once you have become comfortable with looking behind the
many masks you may have been wearing throughout your life, it
becomes evident that the *who* you really are has been there all
along, lingering, patiently awaiting the moment you begin to
peel away the "BS" (Belief System) that has concealed it for so
long. Your authentic self has been your silent partner, your traveling companion, since the day you were born, just waiting for

the appropriate (re)defining moment(s) to occur that would re-mind you it was there. So the real question is, are you revealing your authentic self to the world or keeping it neatly tucked in your back pocket to be pulled out only on special occasions when it is safe or convenient? Knowing where and how to access your authentic self is a wonderful thing, but unless you learn how to give it a voice in your *daily* life, it is all for naught. The practice is to understand there is no area of your life where it is not pres-ent and to consciously weave it into the tapestry of every day. In this process, you'll discover what is known as your authentic voice. The operative words that will help access and express your authentic voice are *trust, courage,* and *consistency.*

Your Authentic Voice Is Not Just Words That Come Out of Your Mouth

"In life, finding a voice is speaking and living the truth. Each of you is an original. Each of you has a distinctive voice. When you find it, your story will be told. You will be heard."
—John Grisham

In literal terms, you can access your voice by means of the sounds that come out of your mouth, but your authentic voice is not just how you use your vocal cords—your authentic voice is how you naturally and seamlessly express the totality of who you are at the center of your being, bringing it to the surface of life by means of your words, deeds, and actions. In other words, your authentic voice is how you show up in your daily life based on your intention to live out loud—to simply be who you know yourself to be. Your authentic voice is not just the delivery system for the words you speak; it's also how you bring the authentic truth of who you are to life every day in every way—it's how you express the sum of your being unflinchingly to the world in such a way that the true you is *seen* as well as *heard*. Once you have found your authentic voice, the practice is to consistently integrate it into your daily life.

Have you noticed that when you suppress your authenticity based on the "appropriateness" of the occasion, you tend to behave differently with strangers or work associates than you may with close friends or family? If you examine this closely, you'll see that you may be taking one persona to work, another to the grocery store, another to the doctor's office, another to church, and yet a different one through the front door of your home at the end of the day. Using the metaphor of the masks that conceal your authentic self, think of it this way: you may slip on one mask to go to a party where you know no one and put on a different mask when you are talking over the fence with your neighbor, each mask concealing the authentic self to different degrees, relevant to how safe you feel in revealing yourself in each situation. This is living horizontally on the surface of life with no sense of connection to the ancient roots that link with the Original Self. Living in this manner, can you imagine the number of (re)defining moments you may have skipped by without even realizing it? One of the telltale signs of one who has completely embraced their authentic self is that they are, *with great consistency*, the same person in public as they are behind closed doors. But don't confuse authenticity with intimacy: authenticity is the ability to consistently be who you really are regardless of where you are or with whom. Intimacy determines the degree of how much of your personal self and life you will reveal to others based on your relationship with them. In other words, you can be equally authentic (real) with a stranger as you would be your lover, but clearly the level of intimacy will be different.

Authenticity and Consistency Go Together

"Who you are speaks so loudly I can't hear what you're saying."

—RALPH WALDO EMERSON

Being the same person on Saturday night you are on Sunday morning is the practice of living so consciously and transparently that your soul, head, heart, mouth, and feet are all aligned and moving, with great consistency, in the same direction at the same time. Through it all, it is your authentic voice that does the talking—not with just your words, but your actions as well. The benefit of expressing your authentic voice with consistency is that you'll never have to wonder who you really are, nor will other people have to wonder who you are—it is self-evident by your mere presence because your authenticity is energetically felt by others. As the saying goes, sometimes actions speak louder than words. In this state of consciousness, you'll notice that your (re)defining moments will be far subtler. Because you have begun to consistently and seamlessly weave your awareness of the presence of your authentic self into the present moment, you won't need drama or fireworks to open the portal to your (re)defining moments. They will subtly reveal themselves naturally, with grace and ease. This is when you become authentically empowered because you are comfortable in your own skin, which frees you to be present in the moment and let go of any attachment to winning the approval of others. When you know who you truly are and you courageously and consistently live anchored in that awareness, your authentic voice goes before you to announce your coming . . . and it needs no words.

Most of us would agree there is not one human being on this planet who, at some level, does not hunger to authentically be themselves without fear of criticism, punishment, condemnation, ridicule, or being made wrong. When we give in to those fears, we stifle our authentic voice and our own creative process, and there is a place within us that knows we are performing for others and not being true to ourselves. It's as if we are playing a role, hoping the audience loves our song and dance routine. In a manner of speaking, it is a form of self-betrayal. Those who have already arrived at the level of freely and consistently living an authentic life understand what I mean by this because they have courageously walked the gauntlet and have come out on the other side. They survived. They know who they are and have transcended the fear to voice it to the world. In other words, they "perform" for no one.

When You Find Your Authentic Voice, Your Life Ceases Being a Performance

"What if the question is not why I am so infrequently the person I really want to be, but why do I so infrequently want to be the person I really am?"

—Oriah Mountain Dreamer

Using myself as an example may help shed more light on this topic because, being a recovering perfectionist with an addiction to winning everyone's approval, I had covered over my authentic self so well, it was difficult to find what I didn't know was missing. Until I was twenty-three years old, I had no concept of what one's authentic voice was or that I might have one of my very own. My first experience of finding my authentic voice was, perhaps by no mistake, a literal experience as a musician and, more specific, a singer. As mentioned in a prior chapter, through a series of remarkable (re)defining moments in the early 1970s, I serendipitously happened upon a (re)defining moment that put me on the pathway of pursuing a degree in music. At the time, the only option for a vocal major was to become a devotee of classical music with an emphasis in opera. Technically, I had developed a fairly good operatic tenor voice that satisfied my voice coach and professors, but I knew something was missing—namely, my heart. It was missing in action. Nearly two years into the program, I came to grips with the fact that I wasn't enjoying myself because I wasn't "into" that style of music. It didn't feel natural to me; it felt forced and rigid. At my recitals, it became clear to me that I was "performing" for the professors; my performances were perfunctory at best. There was no "juice" in it for me—no joy because, in my heart, I knew I was trying to be someone I wasn't and, as a result, the effervescence of the music that filtered through me didn't sparkle. You could say it was flat—not flat in pitch, but in passion.

Eventually, and surely to the dismay of my professors, I found myself hanging out and playing ever more frequently with folk and rock musicians (what one of my professors referred to as "those unsophisticated noisemakers"), many of whom were playing nightly in smoke-filled coffeehouses and bars. It was difficult to face my professors because it felt as if I was living two different lives—and that was the problem; *I was,* and I knew it. This was a real dilemma for me because I knew that eventually I would have to "face the music," as it were. It really wasn't that I was being unfaithful to anyone else; it was that I was being unfaithful to myself, and that was a challenging reality to have to accept. However, fully owning that fact was when my heart cracked opened and soared, albeit while singing in some less-than-savory bars and clubs late most nights to pay my tuition and living expenses. As a result, my voice took on a raspy quality that made the classical music I was singing during the day even more difficult to perform—not to mention displeasing to my professors. We could say my "inner musician" was conflicted and not very happy. Nonetheless, I stayed the course, finished college, received my BA degree in vocal performance, and never sang another aria. I discovered that, musically, I was trying to put a "less than round peg into a more than square hole." (Pun intended.)

The humorous thing is that for years, there were moments when my cell memory from my classical training would kick in while I was singing with different groups. Right in the middle of a song, suddenly I would sound a bit like I was channeling Pavarotti singing "Proud Mary." Looking back, I am surprised my bandmates could stand it. While I was on the right trail, I had not yet completely found my authentic voice. The interesting thing is, about the time I began my spiritual quest, I also discovered a sweet spot in my voice, and it completely reshaped the timbre and character of my vocals. I suspect that was because I had stumbled upon the pathway back to my authentic self and, in the process, I was slowly discovering that I no longer needed to "perform" for anyone. I just had to be willing to be the instrument through which Spirit flowed with natural grace and ease. I even learned how to breathe differently, naturally, rather than like a bagpipe being squeezed by an angry Scotsman, which made a huge difference in the tonal quality and range of my voice. In short, my authentic voice wrapped itself around my singing voice, and when that happened, my music became real for me rather than a performance to please the audience.

You Are the Instrument

By my own example, can you see where, in your own life, you may be stifling your authentic voice? It's important to remember, it isn't about vocal cords—it's about your soul—it's about opening yourself to be the instrument through which your authentic self naturally, seamlessly reveals its uniqueness to the world. Oddly enough, for me, my authentic voice was initially revealed through my singing and, in the years since, has spilled over into the general manner in which I do life. The more I work at consistently remembering who I really am, the more the real me seamlessly flows through all I do. This is how one's authentic voice functions in daily life: from my public speaking, writing, mentoring, seminars, and workshops, to my relationships, from loved ones to strangers . . . I don't perform for anyone anymore. What you get is who I am; it is simply my authentic voice, the real me, seamlessly showing up in every area of my life. Are there moments when I forget who I really am and go a bit "unconscious"? Sure there are. It's in those times, when I catch myself slumbering on the surface of life, that I take a moment to reconnect with my breathing, which takes me on that vertical plunge to the center of my being. Somehow, conscious, intentional breathing always seems to bring me back to the center, where the authentic self awaits me with open arms. The point is that the opportunity for yet another (re)defining moment presents itself when we make space for it to do so.

> "If you ask me what I came into this life to do, I will tell you: I came to live out loud."
>
> —ÉMILE ZOLA

I share my story with you to make a point about the role your authentic voice plays in bringing all of who you really are from your center to the surface of your life. Until you learn how to access your authentic voice, the uniqueness of who you truly are will never be fully realized. What makes you special (just like everyone else) is that you were placed here on this planet to express the one-of-a-kind being only *you* can be. There is no one else like you; your mission here is to own this truth, and, as Émile Zola put it, "live out loud." Your authentic voice will only be revealed when you are willing to come to the edge of your own uncertainties and fear about needing to make your life a performance for the approval of others—including all your "professors" in the school of life, your friends, family, spouses, partners, teachers, ministers, neighbors, and even strangers. Are you honoring your authentic voice today? Is your authentic self seamlessly emerging in your day-to-day life? Listen to your heart, and you will know.

Your Authentic Voice Will Never
Be Found by Being Normal

"Normal is not something to aspire to, it's something to get
away from."
—Jodie Foster

Perhaps one of the greatest inhibiting factors to accessing our
authentic voice lies in the notion that most of us want to be perceived as normal. Be forewarned, being normal comes with a
litany of limitations that muffle the authentic voice, one of
which is mediocrity. "Normal" people seldom "live out loud"
because it tends to disturb those who are stuck in the same box
they are in. It may seem socially appropriate to be normal, but if
we are not mindful, we can lose our uniqueness in normalcy.
The word *normal* comes from the root word *norm,* which is
defined as "standard, usual, the rule; typical, average, medium,
unexceptional, par for the course, or expected." In other words,
to strive to be normal means to conform to a preexisting pattern
wherein a common denominator established by countless strangers determines the quality and content of your life. If there were
ever a classic example of what living on the surface of life looks
like, this is it. *Your* unique, authentic voice will never be found
in the norm. The antithesis of being normal is being natural.
The word *natural* comes from the Latin word *naturalis,* meaning
"existing in or formed by nature." When we internalize and
actualize the true nature of our being, which is our oneness with
life, it will seamlessly externalize in our lives naturally—in,
through, and as our authentic voice. Something very liberating
happens when we cease trying to be normal and begin to align

with our true nature—we set ourselves free to be who we are and, equally important, who we were uniquely born to be.

Perhaps one of the most unthought-of places to look for proof that normalcy is not natural is found in Mother Nature herself. In nature, "normal" doesn't even exist because it is based on human opinion with a predisposition to either live up to or down to the collective consciousness of the species which, for humankind, is essentially balled up in a massive fear of being singled out as "different." Consider the brightly colored birds, fish, animals, and plants that populate much of the planet. There is little evidence that they hold back on expressing their true nature because they want to be seen as "normal." I have never seen a rose bush working hard at being normal, striving to be just like all the other roses in the garden. Some roses are red, some yellow, some white, some pink, some multicolored, some large, some small, some thorny, some thornless—even those of the exact variety differ in so many unique ways. The rose simply draws on the innate Intelligence that lies within its seed that knows what it is supposed to be and, presto, its beauty is naturally and uniquely revealed to the world. There's no struggle, no pushing, no holding back, no judging itself or the other roses— just a gentle unfolding of what it is.

A flower certainly does not seek the applause of an adoring audience for which to perform and validate its worth. In this context, we might say that the authentic substance of the rose is contained within its seed waiting to be set free—waiting for its (re)defining moment, which is when all the natural elements required to bring forth the blossom come together at the just the right and perfect time; its growing season arrives, the sun shines, the rain falls, and its reason for "being" is brought to fruition. Then, with grace and ease, its petals open to the light and unblushingly unfold as if it were saying, "This is me . . . this is my moment . . . this is who I am . . . and this is what I have come here to be." I would say that is very much living out loud, wouldn't you? Can you relate? Are you as willing as the rose is to live out loud—to truly let your authentic voice be heard and seen? Certainly, if the Universe would imbue a rose with such ability, there must be a message there for you and me: don't strive to be normal—be natural, and your authentic voice will rise like the sun on a beautiful summer's morning and seamlessly shine on all that you do—and, perhaps more so, all that you are.

POINTS TO PONDER AND PERSONALIZE

This is a crucial chapter to assimilate because without the ability to "take your authentic self to the streets" (actualizing who you truly are in your daily life), there is really no point in making the journey. Your authentic voice is the connective tissue that unifies the truth of your being with the action of your doing; it's when the "what" you are and the "who" you are speak as one, which goes far beyond the words we utter. As you go through these points, take time to truly pause and ponder each of them. Try to be sensitive to what may be stirring within. As with the metaphor of the rose, that stirring is your authentic self quietly saying, "Yes . . . this is me . . . this is who I am and was meant to be, and I am ready to live out loud!" If you proceed mindfully, you may witness a (re)defining moment in the making.

• Can you relate with the idea that your authentic voice is more than the words that come out of your mouth—that it is revealed by how you live the totality your life? Can you pinpoint any areas of your life where your authentic self shows up more fully expressed than other areas and, if so, why might that be? Do you express your authenticity based on the occasion or whether it is deemed safe or not to be who you really are? If so, explore what you may be attached to that keeps your authentic voice from seamlessly revealing itself in your daily life.

• Can you identify with the story of how my authentic voice was revealed as I pursued my music differently from what my professors had in mind? Who are the "professors" you might be performing for, and are you willing to endure their disapproval and the potential consequences to access your authentic voice?

• Do you ever catch yourself trying to be "normal" as opposed to being "natural"? Do you see how that could dishonor your own individual uniqueness?

• What are the natural elements that need to come together for your authentic voice to be heard and seen, regardless of who may be watching? The elements that will nurture the nature of your authentic voice are trust, courage, and consistency:

1. **Trust:** *Trust there are no mistakes; you were put here with great intention by an Infinite Intelligence that desires to flow in, through, and as you so that It may be fully expressed in a unique and beautiful manner.*

2. **Courage:** *Have the courage to live out loud because, at the end of the day, you are not performing for anyone else's approval or applause.*

3. **Consistency:** *Be consistent in bringing the true you everywhere you go. It's a matter of remembering who you really are, regardless of where or with whom, and seamlessly weaving the two together.*

✳

CHAPTER 11

Your Body Does Not Define You

There Is No Greater (Re)Defining Moment Than When You Realize You Are Not Your Body

The gift of conscious perception can be an astounding event that happens whenever we realize that it is we, and we alone, who assign meaning and value to whatever our eyes fall upon every moment of every day. This includes the body we see standing in front of us in the mirror every morning. The question is, what do we see?

Life probably does not hand us any more visceral experience of how we mistakenly define ourselves than by means of our physical body. From the day we were born, the message we received from the world was that we are our body. This was the first great lie we were given by means of the collective consciousness of humankind, which has always valued itself from the outside in. It wasn't long after the Original Self consolidated Its massive energy field and squeezed into the carbon suitcase we call our body that we began getting spiritual amnesia—forgetting that we were 100 percent pure Essence, or Spirit, *before* we occupied a body. It was so easy to forget who we really were because the gravitational pull of the flesh was so compelling. Our body was our first point of contact with the world, and from the beginning, it was very demanding—our body told us when *it* wanted something; when *it* was hungry, when *it* was cold, when *it* was experiencing pain as well as pleasure, and so on. So the message early on was, "This body is very important . . . I need to pay close attention to it because it knows how to get what it needs and wants." This is when and how we became lost in our body. Soon enough, with an assist from the egoic-self, the body consumed our true identity and became that which determined how we would survive in the world. In our spiritual amnesia, we became our body and took on its worldly identity, with all its facades, frailties, needs, and wants. As we awaken from our forgetfulness, we'll begin to understand that there is a difference between what we *have* and what we *are*. We *have* a body, but we *are not* our body. Many people think of themselves as a body with a soul, while others understand they are a soul with a body.

> "We are in the habit of identifying ourselves with our bodies.
> The idea that we are this body is deeply entrenched in us. But
> we are not just this body; we are much more than that. The
> idea that 'This body is me and I am this body' is an idea we
> must get rid of. If we do not we will suffer a great deal. We
> are life, and life is far vaster than this body . . ."
> —THICH NHAT HANH, *Your True Home*

While our body was ours from the get-go, it took several years to learn that we were not literally physically connected to our parents, especially our mothers. Then came the conscious separation from Mom and the freedom that comes with it. The older we grew, the more independent we became, and as a result, the more significance the body took on. We entered into yet another relationship with our body—one where it seemed we had more control over it. Over the years, we slowly became cognizant that our body was a vehicle that would go where and do what our minds told it to, never really aware of the role it would increasingly play in how we mistakenly defined ourselves. Overnight, it seems, the body became a focal point for opinions and judgments, both our own as well as those of others. With the ego's help, we began placing labels on our body that would determine its worth and how we would relate with it and the world. The older we grew, the more important our body became, not just as a vehicle to move on the surface of life, from point A to point B, but as the medium through which we would connect socially with the world, finding relevance (and often angst) through relationships and shared experiences. Then one day, it happened. The size and shape of our body began to morph in a way we had not experienced before, and the race was on, literally. As new chemicals coursed through our body, our physical appearance, gender, and sexuality became primary points of interest and, in the process, the basis for how we mistakenly defined ourselves became even more ensconced in the body. The curious thing is, years after our initial introduction to who we really are *not*, we still mistakenly allow the body to define us, even well into our senior years. I propose that it doesn't have to be that way. Perhaps it's time for a (re)defining moment or two. Our body does not define us unless we allow it to. There is no better time than now to prove this is so.

Getting Real with Your Self

"'It doesn't happen all at once,' said the Skin Horse. 'You become. It takes a long time. That's why it doesn't happen often to people who break easily, or have sharp edges, or who have to be carefully kept. Generally, by the time you are Real, most of your hair has been loved off, and your eyes drop out and you get loose in the joints and very shabby. But these things don't matter at all, because once you are Real you can't be ugly, except to people who don't understand.'"
—MARGERY WILLIAMS, *The Velveteen Rabbit*

Long before there were mirrors, human beings seemed to be obsessed with their physical appearance; they would gaze into reflecting pools or highly polished metal just to get a glimpse of themselves. Was this just healthy curiosity, or the beginning of an eternal love/hate affair with the physical garment our authentic self lives in? Since antiquity, it seems people have defined themselves (or have been defined by others) by means of what their body image was. *Beautiful, handsome, sexy, ugly, homely, cute, tall, short, trim, petite, skinny, fat, bald, hairy, old, young, fit, strong, weak, white, black, brown, yellow,* or _____ (fill in the blank) became words that helped shape our identity. Do at least one or more of the aforementioned descriptions fit into how you might have defined yourself until now? I found several that still hook my attention. As Margery Williams so beautifully points out in her story about the Velveteen Rabbit, getting Real is not for the faint of heart because it requires a good deal of stripping away of that which has defined us in the past . . . including our attachment to the body and what it looks like. But where do we look for what is Real if it is not to be found in the form of our physical body? This question sets the stage for a (re)defining moment, and if you are present *in the moment,* you'll see it—or more accurately stated, you feel it coming straight at you. Actually, you won't be able to avoid it.

The Phenomenon of Self-Perception and Projection

"And that Aha! that you get when you see an artwork that really hits you is, 'I am that.' I am the very radiance of energy that is talking to me through this painting."
—Joseph Campbell

It has been said that how you see your world is a reflection of how you see yourself. While at times you may not like what you see in the world, this makes perfect sense because the lens through which you see your world is your own consciousness, which is a collection of your deepest beliefs held in both the conscious and subconscious mind. As the saying goes, as within, so without. This is great news because how you see your world offers instant feedback regarding how you are perceiving yourself—spiritually, emotionally, and physically—in any given moment. As I said, with this awareness, every moment becomes a potential (re)defining moment if you are conscious and present in that moment.

As an example, while the subject matter could be any of the aforementioned qualities of reflecting your current body image, because beauty seems to be something we all tend to appreciate, the question might be, where does beauty *really* exist? This is a very subjective question, so let's start with a little self-inquiry:

when was the last time you were struck by the beauty of a sunset or sunrise? Do you remember the sudden impulse and quickening of your heart the first time you gazed into the beautiful eyes of your significant other? Have you ever been moved to tears by a beautiful piece of music or a special passage in a book you were are reading? These are all different variations on a theme called beauty. What is it that triggers that overwhelming, emotional, beyond-description sensation within? It is your recognition of yourself in that which has moved you. Perhaps the Sufi mystic Rumi surmised it best when he wrote, "If you knew yourself for even one moment, if you could just glimpse your most beautiful face, maybe you wouldn't slumber so deeply in that house of clay. Why not move into your house of joy and shine into every crevice! For you are the secret Treasure-bearer, and always have been. Didn't you know?"

This is how awakening to our oneness with life begins, and it is teeming with abundant (re)defining moments . . . if we have eyes to see them. Beauty doesn't exist in the world—it exists in the mind of the beholder—and the same can be said about any of the other aforementioned descriptions we attach to what we perceive in the world, including our physical body. It becomes manifest through the eye of the beholder, but first, before it can pass through the mind or eye, it must rise up from within the heart. Wherever you see beauty or any other quality that reflects the goodness of life in your world today, understand it is a reflection of who you truly are at your center, far *beyond* your physical body—it's an intrinsic quality that lies within that, when triggered by something "out there," arises within the field of your heart and mind. Again, as within, so without. So the question is, what do you see when you cast your eyes upon the world, because it will be an accurate report card for how you perceive yourself. As Henry David Thoreau wrote, "It's not what you look at that matters, it's what you see." Awakening to this reality can, in itself, open the portal to a (re)defining moment. Your physical body doesn't define you nor can it—how *you* perceive it does.

Do You Perceive Your Body as a Burden or Blessing?

> "Acceptance is the act of embracing what life presents to you with a good attitude. Our bodies are among the most willing and wise teachers of this lesson. Unless you spend a large percentage of your time engaged in out-of-body experiences, your body shows up wherever you are. It can be an ever-present benevolent guide or a lifelong cross to bear. The decision is yours . . ."
>
> —CHERIE CARTER-SCOTT, *If Life Is a Game, These Are the Rules*

While this chapter may appear to be minimizing the importance of your physical appearance or condition when it comes to defining who you really are, it certainly doesn't diminish the fact that the body plays a very essential role in your being who you have come here to be. Have you ever stopped to consider what a blessing it is to have a body at all? This becomes even more obvious when you can see your body as the tool for your evolution as a spiritual being. It is the device with which your soul touches the earth, and it has direct access to an inherent wisdom of its own. If you listen to your body's wisdom, it will teach you much of what you need to know to accomplish your mission on this planet. How so? Your body is the intermediary of your emotions, thoughts, and feelings—it is always trying to tell you what's going on at "headquarters" within, in the mind and heart. It's a wonderful biofeedback system that will guide you to your authentic self if you are willing to pay attention. Your job is to deepen your skillfulness in listening to what the body is reporting to you without believing it is the sum of who you really are. The challenge lies in understanding that you can't do that until you learn to accept, honor, and love the body in which you live today. How does that sit with you? The reason I ask is because this topic is where the rubber meets the road for many of us. Take a moment right now and scan your body for any telltale emotional response to this conversation. Can you feel energy moving? Can you sense a (re)defining moment coming?

Accepting What Is

Throughout my life, I have known a number of people who had been dealt a physical disability of one sort or another that required them to live in a body that had, what would be commonly termed "severe limitations." One such individual was Macy Morris. I met Macy in the fifth grade on my first day of school when the teacher asked him to guide me to the principal's office to register for class. Having just moved to California from the Midwest, I didn't know a single person at school, so Macy became my first friend. As we walked down the hall chatting, I had to move a bit slower than usual. Macy had polio, and he walked with one crutch as he dragged a lifeless leg behind him. I had never known anyone with polio before, and I have to admit, at nine years old, I felt sorry for Macy because I assumed he was missing out on a lot of fun on the playground.

I assumed wrong. At recess, in a game of softball, I was stunned to see Macy slowly move to the batter's box, pick up the bat while leaning on his crutch, and with both hands on the bat, swing and hit the ball. Then he hopped all the way to first base while balancing on the crutch in one hand. After he made it to first base, one of the other kids would "pinch run" for him, and they fought for the honor to do so. Macy was equally aggressive in volleyball, tetherball, and kickball. What I remember so well is that none of the other kids treated Macy any differently from anyone else; it was as if they didn't perceive his "disability." Of course, that was because he did not perceive himself as disabled; Macy didn't define himself by the condition of his body, so how could anyone else? I lost track of Macy after the eighth grade, but he has remained etched in my mind for well over fifty years. I will never forget him as one of my best teachers. He knew he was not defined by his body, and he lived out loud and loved every minute of it.

Countless other people have refused to be defined by their disabilities, many of which happened later in their lives, such as Gabrielle "Gabby" Giffords, the former U.S. Congresswoman who, in January 2011, was shot in the head and nearly died. Following an arduous recovery, she has since, in spite of some permanent "disabilities," returned to the public eye, committed to being a voice in gun control issues that continue to plague the United States. In spite of her injuries, Congresswoman Giffords stands as testimony that we are more than what happens to our bodies. We need look no further than the Wounded Warrior Project or the Paralympic Games to find living, breathing examples of ordinary people who, through extraordinary courage and commitment, continue to prove to themselves and the world that they are not defined by what has happened to their bodies.

If we are teachable, these *extra*ordinary role models prove "accepting what is" with courage and faith is, without question, a choice that can open the portal to a (re)defining moment.

Perhaps the Real Lesson Is to Stop Staring at the Problem

Learning the lesson our body may be offering us is just that, a lesson—it need not define us. The problem is, too often we end up staring so long at the "condition" of the body (resisting it, resenting it, denying it, hiding it, or, at the other end of the spectrum, worshipping it, primping it, adoring it, putting it on display) that we actually breathe the breath of more life into it, which only serves to energize and emphasize the issue we are busy judging. In the process, because it is such a visceral experience, we become even more convinced that the condition or appearance of the body is who we are. In other words, we spend so much time identifying with the form of the body, we lose any sense of the true Self who resides within that form, regardless of its condition. Whether we perceive our body as "less than" or "more than" perfect, the reality is, the ego can have a field day with either perception. As you'll discover, "perfect" is not a condition; it is a state of mind. Accepting "what is" allows you to transcend the egoic-self attachment that comes with identifying too closely with the shell in which you live called your body.

"The body in which your soul self resides at this moment, perhaps with all of its aches and pains, is creating exactly the experience you need to be fully alive as a human being and as a spiritual being. The aliveness and real healing comes in

knowing that it's through fully embracing your humanness
that you find your divinity."

—From *The Art of Being:*
101 Ways to Practice Purpose in Your Life

Embracing our humanness is not always the easiest thing to do,
but it offers us a way to start a healing process that takes us far
beyond the condition. We access our divinity only to the degree
we accept and embrace our humanity on the surface of life. If
your body is giving you fits today, the practice is, to the best of
your ability, not to become entangled in the "Why is this happening to me?" quagmire, but rather to be open to what lies
beyond the quagmire. There is a wisdom body beyond your
physical body that knows nothing about conditions—it knows
only wholeness because that is what it is; wholeness is never defined by conditions—it's a state of being. Despite what the body
of evidence is pointing to, there lies a greater truth behind it.
Breathe into this awareness, and witness how your body re-
sponds to the simple awareness of Presence.

It can be challenging to embrace the idea that your body in
its current condition may have a message for you, especially if
that condition reflects one of illness, malady, or a disability of
some sort. For the purpose of this discussion, what the "condition" may be isn't really the issue; the issue is, will you choose to
allow it to define who you are or choose to see it for what it is—
an experience the body you occupy is currently having. That
perspective alone may open you to a (re)defining moment. Perhaps the message has to do with treating your body with more
respect and reverence, making sure it receives what it needs to
continue serving you in a manner that allows you to do what is
yours yet to do. To objectify this point, consider your body as

your automobile because, spiritually speaking, that is what it is—a vehicle your soul-self leased to ride in on its journey through the terrain of the human condition. While you know you are not your car, you still ensure it is serviced, fueled, and cleaned properly and regularly, don't you? Why would you treat your body any less mindfully? On the other hand, perhaps the message your body has for you is not about needing to change it at all, but rather making peace and accepting "what is," which frees you to make the best of the situation. The point in either case is to be clear that your body (or its current condition) is not who you truly are. The practice is to remember that while your body doesn't define who you are, as long as you are living in it, love it.

How Old Would You Be If You Didn't Know How Old You Were?

"Nobody grows old merely by living a number of years. We grow old by deserting our ideals. Years may wrinkle the skin, but to give up enthusiasm wrinkles the soul."

—SAMUEL ULLMAN

My dad recently celebrated his ninety-third birthday. I called him to wish him happy birthday, but he was busy "working out" on the treadmill so I had to call back later. When I finally talked to him, I said, "So, Pop, what are you doing to celebrate your special day?" Without missing a beat, he replied, "Breathing." After we both stopped laughing, he said he was spending the day learning more about his new high-speed computer (which my siblings and I gave him for Father's Day). His latest project, between sessions Skyping with his old cronies online, is researching the Jones family heritage on Ancestor.com. His energy and enthusiasm for life continue to amaze me; he is very much like the Energizer Bunny—he just keeps going and going. If there was ever a poster child for the "My age does not define me" club, this is the guy.

I say the following with the greatest of respect for those who have worked hard to maintain a fit and youthful-looking body: it's important to be able to delineate the difference between doing these things to preserve the "appearance" of your body because we fear losing social approval and the external power our youth brought to us, and doing them simply because it helps us feel better about ourselves. What differentiates the two? The first is about our *exterior* and relates to how we define ourselves, and the second is about our *interior* and relates to a quality of life. I know this is a slippery slope, but it is, nonetheless, an important one to be traveled. Throughout our current history, we, as a culture, have been waging war against aging. We desire anything that promises to preserve the body and make it "appear" younger than it is. The message is quite clear: there is something wrong with being who we are by aging naturally. No one wants their body to get old. Perhaps that is because we, as a society, have essentially devalued our elders—so much so that those approaching their senior years fight against the unavoidable consequences of living in an aging body because no one in their right mind wants to be discounted and pushed aside based solely on their age. This message is so deeply inculcated in our collective mind that many people in their twenties and thirties are way ahead of the curve, leading the battle against natural aging in order to delay the inevitable as long as possible.

Of course, behind all this lies the mistaken belief that the age of the body in which we live defines who we are. Whether we are young or old, we should not be seduced into believing that the age of our body has even the slightest effect on the true Self that lives within our body. The Life Force that sustains one's body knows nothing about how old we are. One of the things I love most about my dad is that, although his body may be ninety-three years old, his mind is still young. Because I have always looked to him as a role model, over the years, I have studied him, wondering how he has managed to maintain such a vital life force, and this is what I have learned from him:

- He doesn't complain. Ever. Even when I was a kid, I noticed that, regardless of what may have been going on in his life—and there were some challenging times— when anyone asked how he was doing, his answer would usually be something like, "If I were any better I would be two" . . . or, "This is a great day to be alive."
- He doesn't criticize. He looks for the best in people and praises it.
- He doesn't hold grudges. He is quick to forgive and move on.
- He remembers to tell those he cares about and loves that he cherishes them and demonstrates it with bear hugs and kisses.
- He expresses his gratitude for the gift of life every day and takes no one and nothing for granted.
- He continues to grow and keep his mind agile by adding new content to it.
- He stays connected to his soul. He knows who he is, and spirituality is as natural to him as breathing. He honors and respects his body as if it were a living temple for the Divine because he knows it is.

I suppose the list could go on, but I trust you get my point.
This really isn't so much about my dad as it is the potential he
demonstrates you and I have to live a long, purposeful, fulfilling, and joyful life that is not defined by the age of the body
we occupy. As we age, the practice is to remember that perspective really is everything. In the words of George Burns,
"You can't help getting older, but you don't have to get old."
To that, I say, amen.

What Sex Is Your Authentic Self?

"When we touch the place in our lives where sexuality and
spirituality come together, we touch our wholeness and the
fullness of our power, and at the same time our connection
with a power larger than ourselves."

—JUDITH PLASKOW

What sex are you? Perhaps the more accurate question is, what
sex is your body? As you consider this question, notice how
quickly your mind scrambles to put a label on you. Now, working from a premise that you are not your body, what sex would
you say your authentic self is? To ask what sex your authentic self
is, is rather like asking what sex the Universe is. The answer is
neither. Because the true Self existed as that divine spark of the
Infinite *before* It individuated and set up home in your body, it is
impossible to assign It a gender. In other words, your true Original Self is genderless. However, upon arrival, your soul—the
spiritual aspect of your authentic self that *knows* it is on a mission
to reconnect with the Source from which it came—intentionally
choose the body you live in based, in part, upon its gender,

knowing it would provide the perfect opportunities for the soul to unfold.

Your soul has a predisposition to creating the most appropriate pathways leading to the lessons it requires for its own evolution. The body you live in is the form and your sexuality is one of many aspects that serve the needs of your soul in that process; it sets in motion the dynamics by means of which, eventually, and perhaps with much trial and tribulation, you'll realize that you are not your body, but something far greater. While your sex was determined by genetics and the anatomy with which you were born, your sexuality is one of the most significant ways the expression of "what you are" (pure spirit) manifests through the "who you are" (a body with many labels, including gender) in your daily life. The practice is to learn how to get comfortable with your sexuality because, although it does not define who you truly are, as long as you live in your body, you will still have to contend with the fact you are a sexual being.

> "We are all born sexual creatures, thank God, but it's a pity
> so many people despise and crush this natural gift."
> —MARILYN MONROE

There is perhaps no single aspect of living in a human body where we may be more compelled to mistakenly believe that we are our body than when it comes to our sexuality. Because the energy and impulse for sexual expression becomes so wedded with the body, it commands our attention perhaps more hours of the day than we may realize. The packaging and selling of sexuality is the single biggest industry in the world. This industry knows how to tap into our innate sex drive and use it to its advantage. Just watch television for an hour and count the innuendoes, inferences, images, and words that are sexually oriented. If not included in the program itself, you'll discover that a majority of the commercials use some level of sex appeal to sell their products. I am not passing judgment here. I enjoy sex, and I trust that almost every adult does (or has at some point in their life) as well. I merely want to point out that, along with our inborn natural sex drive, we are so bombarded, subliminally and overtly, with sexually explicit messages, it has become second nature for us to think of ourselves as a body that has a gender with physical and emotional needs and desires, as well as a need to *be* desired.

From an early age, many people begin to identify so thoroughly with their sexuality (and the physical body that serves as its instrument) that it defines them—and all the while their authentic self lies waiting patiently for that (re)defining moment to occur when they are given an opportunity to look more deeply within, beyond gender, beyond sexual preferences, and beyond the desires, needs, and appearance of the physical form. The practice is to learn how to love the entirety of *who* you are, with all its mistakenly perceived flaws, as well as the wholeness of *what* you are with all Its absolute perfection. Read on, and perhaps you'll understand what I mean and how to do it as well.

Fully Accepting Yourself—Warts, Wrinkles, and All—Is a (Re)defining Moment in the Making

". . . imagine practicing just Being in front of a camera. What a great tool and moment of opportunity to be present with any old thoughts that surface telling you that you're not enough. Concerns that you're too fat, too thin, that your nose is too big, too small, that you have too many wrinkles, or that your smile is not flattering. The list goes on and on. How would it be to completely love yourself for exactly who you are in that One Frame at a Time moment . . . ?"

—CARL STUDNA, *Click!*

I don't know about you, but I really have a difficult time sitting still, holding that uncomfortable "posed smile" for the photographer because that single moment before the "click" seems to go on for a very long time. It always makes me feel just a bit phony. Have you noticed the photographer never says, "Just look natural for the camera"? It's usually, "Okay . . . smile for the camera" and that is what I have the greatest problem with—smiling on command. I generally have a sunny disposition, but the microsecond just before the "click" of the camera nearly always catches me between smiles, with my eyes blinking, squinting, or gazing off into the distance, essentially doing anything to escape the dreaded freeze-frame moment. I had seldom wondered why I disliked having my picture taken so much until I read *Click!* by my friend Carl Studna. Now I think I know why: the camera doesn't lie—it looks right into us and offers us real-time feedback, an opportunity to pause and see who we perceive ourselves to be between "perfect poses," and perhaps, even about how we really feel about ourselves in that moment.

Isn't It a Shame?

I have long believed we live in a shame-based society that seems quite adept at reminding us of our self-perceived flaws and shortcomings. To help put shame into perspective, consider the difference between kissing cousins, shame and guilt. It has been said that guilt is a feeling or belief that we have *made* a mistake; shame is a feeling or belief that we fundamentally *are* a mistake, which renders us "in-valid" and sends us on a scavenger hunt for whole-ness, looking everywhere for what's missing (on the surface of life), other than the only place we'll ever find it—within. In other words, the hidden toxic energy around shame is buried in a belief that we are not "enough" just the way we are and the tendency when we feel incomplete is to seek our "enough-ness" wherever we can find it.

Main Street, USA, has made it its business to keep us feeling less than whole—that is, until we buy what they are selling, including other people's opinions of what makes us good enough, smart enough, desirable enough, rich enough, popular enough, healthy enough, or _____ (fill in the blank) enough. I mention this because what Studna points out in his book is that if we are able to lean into the awkwardness of being in front of the metaphorical camera of daily life with a willingness to love ourselves "enough" to be who we authentically are—warts, wrinkles, and all—the snapshot of the moment will always yield a reflection of our true wholeness, despite what the critics and marketers have to say. There is no feeling we can ever have that will bring greater satisfaction than that of wholeness because it is the effect of completely and unconditionally loving ourselves and our life, just the way we are, and the way it is, with no "yeah, but"s attached. Wholeness is not a condition or a point at which we one day arrive when everything about us is perfect, because that day will never come. Wholeness is a state of being. It's about remembering to remember that we are not defined by our body, ever, even on special occasions when the egoic-self pops up unexpectedly.

The takeaway for me is this: arriving at a point of authentic self acceptance frees us to show up in those "click" moments with no need to be perfect, which alone is a major accomplishment and relief for most of us. Being a recovering perfectionist, I know from whence I speak. If you can relate with this conversation, below is an exercise I invite you to try. If you do this process with clear intention and an open heart, you may find that it leads to—you guessed it—yet another opportunity to experience a (re)defining moment:

- Ask someone you are comfortable with to take your photograph.
- As you sit waiting for the "click," conduct a quick scan of how you are feeling about yourself in that moment. Rather than looking into the camera lens, allow your gaze and facial muscles to soften naturally and focus your thoughts on your heart center, breathing slowing and deeply.
- Consider the gift of life that was unconditionally given to you so many years ago. Then think about how much you must have been loved—so much so that the Original Self clothed Itself in this garment called "your body."
- Finally, allow a sense of gratitude for the gift to rise gently from your heart center and reveal itself on your face. When the "click" comes, you'll see a reflection of the authentic self you really are in that photograph, and that really is a beautiful thing to behold.

If you are at all challenged with this process, consider asking yourself the question Carl Studna proposes: "How would it be to completely love myself for exactly who I am in this One Frame at a Time moment?" You might want to add to that, "How would

it be to love myself for exactly *what* I am?" Can you love the totality of your being that much—your physical body and your true
Self—just one moment at a time? Knowing that you are not defined by your body should make loving it much easier—warts,
wrinkles, and all. The practice is to remember that you need your
body as much as it needs you to exist; it's a true partnership. But
never forget who is in charge. Finding your way back to the authentic self is your mission, and your body is the vehicle that
makes the journey possible. Learn to love the vehicle and enjoy
riding in it, but never mistake it for who you truly are.

POINTS TO PONDER AND PERSONALIZE

• How does the idea that you are not your body fit into
your current belief system? Have you ever contemplated
your body as a vehicle in which your soul-self travels,
gathering soul-expanding experiences?

• Do you ever catch yourself categorizing your body as
beautiful, handsome, ugly, homely, cute, tall, short,
trim, petite, skinny, fat, bald, hairy, old, young, over-
weight, strong, weak, disabled, and so on? If so, can you
see how doing so day after day, year after year, might
lead to defining yourself from the outside in rather than
the inside out?

• Do you perceive your body as a burden or a blessing?
The practice is to remember these two things:

1. *While your body is not the totality of who you are, it is, nonetheless, the only one you'll be issued for this journey.*
2. *Your body is the sole (and soul) means by which your authentic self touches the earth.*

Remembering these two things may help you seek and find the blessings of your body rather than focusing on what you may not like about it.

- Can you pinpoint any specific areas of your life where you may be giving too much power to your body image, allowing it to be that which defines you in the world? This includes the color of your skin, the shape, size, and age of your body. The practice is to remember that none of it represents the truth of your being; underneath your body image lies the authentic self, and it only knows itself as unconditional love. There is no greater (re)defining moment than when you realize you are *not* your body, but you *are* one with the love that sustains it.

As a Mindfulness Practice, Consider the Following:

1. Stand or sit in front of a mirror, and connect with your breath.

2. As you begin to feel anchored in your breathing, look into and not just at the body reflected in the mirror.

3. Begin to peel away the obvious things you notice, such as the shape of your body, the color and condition of your skin, your facial hair, the color and shape of your eyes. Continue to peel away the labels, including your gender and age.

4. Now, softly gaze into your eyes and stay connected to your breath. As you go deeper, allowing yourself the gift of nonjudgmental connection, silently ask yourself, Who is in there? Beyond all of these layers of "body," who lives in there? If your attention drifts, gently call it back and align with your breath. If it helps, think of this process as taking the vertical pilgrimage from the surface of your life into the center of your being where the "who" meets the "what."

5. Continue asking, Who lives in there? until all the layers (labels) have been peeled away and the answer is crystal clear: "Ah . . . this is the essence of the Original Self looking at Itself . . . loving Itself." Stay with this sense of oneness for as long as you can and then say, "Thank you for reminding me who I truly am. I am not just this body, but something far more amazing. I am a spark of infinite Life, knowing itself and loving itself as me . . . as this body . . . as this mind . . . and as this soul, just the way I am."

6. Finally, realize you have just opened the portal to a (re)defining moment. Now breathe, smile, and be at peace.

CHAPTER 12

Forgiveness Can Be a (Re)Defining Moment

It's Impossible for the Authentic Self to Hold a Grudge

The wound is the place where the Light enters you.
—RUMI

Life, it seems, is always giving us opportunities to grow our roots more deeply into the subterranean soil where the authentic self awaits us, and much to our chagrin, it is not always the pathway of sunshine, blue skies, and green lights. Often it is through our greatest pain, rather than our greatest pleasures, that we find our way back to the Original Self from which we came. Kahlil Gibran echoed these sentiments perfectly when he wrote, "Your pain is the breaking of the shell that encloses your understanding. Even as the stone of the fruit must break, that its heart may stand in the sun, so must you know your pain." Sometimes it's the deepest wounds we suffer that can open us to receive the guidance we need to stay on the pathway. The pain to which I am referring is not necessarily held in the physical body alone, but also in the emotional body, where it wraps itself around invisible wounds such as resentment, anger, and bruised feelings.

The good news is, if we are conscious and present when that wound is inflicted, it can open the portal to a (re)defining moment. We can allow the pain of that wound to lead us to the sacred depths within where the Light of infinite Presence illumines the way to our center—through the heart—to the sacred place where the authentic self resides. (Note: the word *Light* is capitalized in this chapter to denote it is synonymous with the true Self.) The operative words here are *conscious* and *present*, which is not always what and where we are when our reactive self (or egoic-self) is at the helm. This is when we tend to take things personally and begin immediately to "build a case" to justify why we feel or act the way we do. Then we seal that case so tightly that no Light can possibly penetrate it and tuck away the experience in a shadowy corner of our mind where it becomes a brewery for toxic emotions, simmering until one day they have no choice but to burble up and manifest in our body and the body of our affairs. This is not to say that many of us who have carried wounds inflicted by others are not fully justified in feeling resentful or angry. The question is, do we want to stay stuck in resentment—in that toxic brew, allowing it to fester? Is it serving us in creating a life of wholeness and happiness—a life worth living? In other words, regardless of how we received the wounds, are we *willing* to let them go for *our* own highest and greatest good? I have known people who were so severely stuck in the darkness of their resentment that their physical bodies were disease-ridden but still they were not interested in exploring the relationship between the resentment they clung to and their body, which was in rapid descent and decay—and to what end? It doesn't have to be that way.

If we are mindful and *willing* to step beyond the shadow of resentment, we'll be able to see the portal to a (re)defining moment opening directly ahead. Rumi's words are profound and prophetic when he states, "The wound is the place where the Light enters you." However, taking a little poetic license, I would like to embellish this pearl of wisdom by adding, ". . . *if* you allow it to." In truth, the Light is *already* within because it comes from your center, not the surface of life. The wound Rumi speaks of creates the opening through which the Light can be experienced if we are willing to stand in its radiance. The good news is, there is a powerful and holistic way for our invisible wounds to be permanently healed if we are but willing to pull back the blinds of a tightly sealed mind, open the window of our heart, take a deep and cleansing breath, and let the Light Rumi speaks of into our field of awareness. Forgiveness is the practice that opens the window and exposes our wounds to the Light, and it is a practice that, as long as we live in a human skin, we'll have a need to employ throughout our lives. The practice is to remember that before we can forgive, we must become consciously aware that there is a need for forgiveness. Many of us have been dragging the invisible wound of resentment (and its cousins, hate and anger) with us for such a long time, we have become desensitized to it, and it has created a home in the infrastructure of our lives without our conscious awareness.

Dragging the Past into the Present to Build Your Future Is Not Always a Wise Call

"When we think we have been hurt by someone in the past, we build up defenses to protect ourselves from being hurt in the future. So the fearful past causes a fearful future and the past and future become one. We cannot love when we feel fear. When we release the fearful past and forgive . . . we will experience total love and oneness with all."

—GERALD G. JAMPOLSKI

The Colosseum in Rome was originally built in A.D. 70. It is estimated that approximately 500,000 people and more than a million wild animals died in the Colosseum games over the centuries—no doubt a tremendous source of pain and suffering. From a historical perspective, it holds more than a few lessons for us to garner about its past—as well as our own. In spite of its violent history (and perhaps because of it), the Colosseum is an imposing edifice to behold, even in its present state. If you have seen it, either in person or in photographs, you have no doubt noticed that a large part of it no longer exists. What I learned was that while a number of fires and earthquakes over the centuries helped deconstruct and decommission the Colosseum, its eventual demise was not due solely to Mother Nature. Nor was it caused by poor or inferior building materials. Ironically, just the opposite. During and after the medieval ages, it became a pilferer's paradise. Throughout the ensuing centuries, two-thirds of the stones, metal, and lumber that made up the massive arena were eventually pulled apart, dragged away, and used as building materials for other projects far and wide. (As an example, the steps of St. Peter's in Rome are made of reused Colosseum stones.) In short, people were "recycling" old materials from the past to build their future. I am a proponent of recycling when and where we can to help preserve our environment, but the metaphor here is just too juicy to pass up: certain aspects of the Colosseum represent our personal history—some of which may be filled with painful memories inflicted by the cruelty and thoughtlessness of others that we continue to drag along with us, day after day, year after year, where they become building blocks for more of the same in the future. Rather than learning from the past, through resentment and judgment, we keep it very much alive in the present, where it becomes cause to more of the same in the future. The moral of the story is simple: we have to master the practice of not dragging our past into the present unless it serves our future in a positive and constructive way, like the Colosseum stones used to create the steps of St. Peter's.

Your History Doesn't Have to Become the Hi-Story That Defines You

It is vital to remember that if we are not conscious and present in the moment, we can still have defining moments, but they are not necessarily positive ones. They can actually pull us into the vortex of a downward spiral in our evolutionary process.

For millennia, human beings have been defining themselves based on their interactions with the world rather than from an internal knowing of the true Self. Negative encounters with other human beings, which end up as a primary ingredient in the toxic stew of resentment, are *always* anchored in the past and then dragged along into the present moment, where they get embellished, magnified, and projected into the future, finding new life in an endless loop of cause and effect. This is not only true for us as individuals but as a society. If we look at the history our own species, hate, anger, and resentment have been passed down from one generation to the next based on something that happened centuries ago, years ago, or even days ago. Countries do it, religions do it, ethnicities do it; in short, people do it. When we perceive our past negative experiences through the prism of resentment, we keep them alive in the present moment where, both consciously and unconsciously, they continue to burble, boil, and brew in the stew that contaminates our life. By dwelling on them—or, worse yet, repeatedly talking about them—our resentments become the predominate story that helps shape who we think we are (a victim) without our conscious awareness that it is even happening. And the world can't help but see us the way we see ourselves. When we turn our history into our "hi-story," it becomes how we are defined in the world. And here's the hook: through the law of cause and effect, the Universe conspires to support us in justifying how we feel by creating an ongoing series of circumstances that render unto us more of the same. Unconditional forgiveness is the intention behind the energy that opens the wound, beckons the Light Rumi speaks of, and breaks that repetitive cycle—but we have to be conscious and present to initiate the process.

Again, being *conscious* and *present* in the moment are operative words when it comes to taking the vertical plunge and accessing the authentic self. Being conscious and present allows us to become witness to our own healing process, which is a prerequisite to living an authentic life and making wiser choices, responding appropriately rather than reacting inappropriately. Negative emotions such as anger and resentment conceal the true Self in the same way cloudy skies conceal the sun; although the sun is always there, the clouds must be blown away so it may reveal its light to us. Forgiveness is the gentle breeze that removes the clouds of judgment that separate us from our deepest self, which, in turn, allows the Light to flood in through our wounds where all things are made whole in the presence of the Infinite One. So where, when, and how do we begin to detoxify the energy of anger, hate, and resentment through forgiveness? Read on—perhaps there is a (re)defining moment ahead in the form of an old wound through which the Light may serve as a guide—if you are willing to follow Its lead.

> "An eye for an eye only ends up making the whole world blind."
>
> —MAHATMA GANDHI

For some people, any mention of forgiveness simply chafes and agitates them because they are preoccupied with the notion that revenge is the only option and action warranted when they have somehow been wronged—it's all about payback. This is the "eye for an eye" mentality to which Mahatma Gandhi was referring to and, unfortunately, it is endemic in much of our species. For the most part, these are generally people who can't "see" that they are living on the surface of life (meaning they have no sense of being connected to something larger than themselves) and, therefore, forgiveness is not on their radar. It's not even a word in their regular vocabulary—it is a foreign concept and makes no sense because it implies vulnerability and weakness that lead to defeat and loss. These people see the physical world as a threat and are not comfortable in exploring outside that box.

In his seminal book, *The Seat of the Soul,* Gary Zukav shares the idea that we perceive the world through either the eyes of "love and trust or fear and doubt." Clearly, judgment and a sense of separation from others is based in fear and doubt and is the energy that fortifies the walls of that box. For people who live their lives from the inside out (meaning they live from their center in an awareness that they are one with something sacred, something far greater than themselves), forgiveness comes as a natural impulse. Why? They see the world through the eyes of love and trust; they live closer to the hub of the wheel of life, where everyone and everything is interconnected with the sacred thread of life. We can learn to live our lives through love and trust or fear and doubt. One moves us ever closer to the center of our being and, therefore, closer to who we truly are; the other compels us to surface living, where taking things personally is a way of life. Which will you choose?

What My Dog Taught Me about Forgiveness

One night, when I was lying on the floor working out with my hand weights, unbeknownst to me, my dog (and master teacher), MacDoodle, walked up behind me and stood directly in the path of an ascending weight and got whacked on the side of his head. He stood there dazed for a moment as I apologized profusely. Then he looked at me with those amazing big brown puppy-dog eyes, wagged his tail, licked my face, laid down, and took a nap. He didn't spend even one moment pouting or trying to lay a guilt trip on me. My human nature interpreted that as his way of saying, "I forgive you," because a half hour later we were out in the yard playing with Mr. Frisbee as if nothing had ever happened. I believe that is because, *in his mind*, nothing did happen—he had totally forgotten the experience of being bonked in the head because he was busy exploring the possibilities to play that the current moment held.

There is a great lesson here for those of us who tend to hold on to resentment from past hurtful experiences. It robs us of the gift of being fully present in the moment, which is where life is waiting for us to fully engage in being who we came here to be. However, dealing effectively with the negative energy of resentment seems to be a skill that most humans are still working to get a handle on. If there is anything I have learned from my teacher MacDoodle, it is this: things happen to all of us that cause pain and suffering—often by accident, sometimes by thoughtless people with malevolent intent. In either case, holding on to resentment and anger about what has happened only keeps us stuck in the past where we are powerless to create anything new.

"Stuff happens" that we may or may not have control over, but the one thing we do have absolute control over is how we respond or react. This is the power of conscious and present-minded choice. This action alone helps shape our destiny, and I mean this literally: numerous medical studies suggest there is a strong link between long-held resentment, which is anger in disguise, and the damage it does to our physical bodies and emotional well-being. As the Buddha reportedly once said, you will not be punished for your anger; you will be punished by your anger. Whether he actually said it or not is secondary to the fact that the sentiment is accurate; the energy of anger and resentment eats away at our minds, our bodies, and the body of our relationships. Given this knowledge, the question has to be, why would anyone want to intentionally hold on to resentment, regardless of how justified it may be? Is it possible that the idea of forgiveness frightens us?

Forgiveness Is Not for the Faint of Heart

"The weak can never forgive.
Forgiveness is the attribute of the strong."

—Mahatma Gandhi

It is imperative to understand that the practice of unconditional forgiveness is not meant to diminish the fact that many of us may have legitimate reasons to be angry toward another person or persons, and this is also not to say that we can't be victimized by other people, because we most certainly can be. I have heard some boldly declare, "There are no victims, only volunteers." I would counsel them, while speaking in platitudes and absolutes, to infuse a bit more compassion in their comments. Relatively speaking, we only need to look at the world in which we live to see what could be labeled as "unforgivable" acts of brutality, terrorism, murder, physical or sexual abuse, embezzlement, fraud, infidelity—and the list could go on. Who in their right mind would deny that being a victim of such things doesn't warrant anger and resentment toward the perpetrators? Being subjected to such suffering is a tangible wound to the one who is victimized and, thus, should be dealt with compassionately. But here is where the slope can get very slippery: anyone can be victimized, but *remaining* a victim by clinging to the past and dragging it along behind us, day after day, year after year, is a choice we make.

Anger Isn't Really the Problem;
Resentment Is

Let us be clear here that we are not demonizing anger—it's what we do with it that matters. Anger can be a healthy thing if it is expressed in an appropriate and proactive manner. Anger can be a creative energy; the question is, what shall it create? When dealt with mindfully and proactively, anger can be a powerful mobilizing factor that results in positive change. When dealt with reactively and mindlessly, however, it can create great destruction, which, at the end of the day, causes suffering for everyone. When we address anger in a conscious and proactive manner, the energy caused by a certain occurrence or event is defused as its purpose is being served—its energy has been spent in a healthy way. Resentment, on the other hand, is the clinging to and regeneration of anger caused by that event, "re-sent" through our minds and bodies on a continual basis, which is when it becomes our master and ultimate destroyer. People we "hold" in resentment are actually "holding" us prisoners in a mental and emotional jail they created but we maintain. Even more ironic is that, in many cases, the people we hold in resentment don't even know or care—or worse yet, some of them have long been gone. But here we are, still allowing them to hold us hostage to a past that no longer exists, and all the while, we are the one holding the key to the cell door. That key is, of course, forgiveness. When we awaken to this truth, we set ourselves free, the cell door is flung open, and we step into a (re)defining moment that has been there all along, just waiting for us to turn the key.

At the end of the day, forgiveness is really not for the other person's benefit at all—it's for our own. Regardless of how il-

logical it may seem at times, it is through unconditional forgiveness that we surrender the past to the past and enter the present,
freeing ourselves to stand in the infinite Light that knows how
to heal our deepest and most painful wounds. It is in this context
that I say the act forgiveness is not for the faint of heart because
it can require a tremendous amount of strength and courage to
strip ourselves naked of all defenses, excuses, and righteousness
and expose ourselves to the brilliance of the Light Rumi refers
to. If this action doesn't open the portal to a profound (re)defin-
ing moment, perhaps nothing ever will. Forgiveness is definitely
an attribute of an authentic being—one who is strong in spirit
and yet emotionally flexible enough to bend with the breeze
that clears the mind, opens the heart, and gently invites Light to
enter their wound. An authentically empowered being knows
that forgiveness frees them from the shackles of the past—if they
are willing to just let go of what was and open to what can be in
a new day.

Today Really Is the First
Day of the Rest of Your Life

> "He allowed himself to be swayed by his conviction that
> human beings are not born once and for all on the day their
> mothers give birth to them, but that life obliges them over
> and over again to give birth to themselves."
> —GABRIEL GARCÍA MÁRQUEZ

In the Scriptures, Paul says our lives can "be transformed by the
renewing of our mind." Have you ever wondered what it takes
to renew one's mind? Again, Paul offers an answer to that question when he says, "I die daily." To die daily is to allow each

day to be done—finished—complete—kaput when your head hits the pillow with a commitment not to drag yesterday into the new day ahead. While it is a metaphor, "to die daily" means you must be willing to give birth to yourself over and over with each new sunrise, knowing that in so doing, you are stepping into the creative field of infinite mind, where all possibilities for new life exist. John Wayne summarized this sentiment beautifully when he said, "Tomorrow is the most important thing in life. Comes into us at midnight very clean. It's perfect when it arrives and it puts itself in our hands. It hopes we've learned something from yesterday."

Using either St. Paul or John Wayne's inspired words, can you see the necessity of forgiveness in the process of being renewed daily? A simple understanding of the law of cause and effect affirms that when you enter a new day with a new mind, you create a new life. Forgiveness, as a daily practice, allows you to awaken each day spiritually and emotionally clean—renewed and realigned with the authentic self you came here to be. Do you remember the old saying, "Today is the first day of the rest of your life"? Believe it, and make good use of it, because it ends at midnight. Welcome to your new life . . . again. Forgiveness is not just a practice; it is the way to a (re)defining moment.

Points to Ponder and Personalize

- How do you respond to the topic of forgiveness? Did you notice any resistance in your mind or body to the idea that forgiveness is one of many necessary practices for the person who wishes to experience the possibility of a (re)defining moment?

- Can you see how clinging to resentment, anger, and hate acts as an invisible force field that separates the human you and your authentic self? You cannot experience the authentic self and resentment at the same time. Which do you believe holds the greatest future for you? Or perhaps better said—which serves you better in the process of "becoming who *you* were born to be"?

- Could you relate with the metaphor of the Colosseum in Rome? Have you been dragging any past pain and suffering into the present that have become building blocks for more of the same in the future?

- How does the idea of unconditional forgiveness fit into your belief system? True forgiveness means forgiving everyone; it means granting absolution for everyone, including yourself, who has wronged you—and not just those who may have "earned forgiveness." Hard to do? Of course it is, which is why the "eye-for-an-eye" mind-set has endured for millennia. Possible to do? Yes. Absolute forgiveness is guided by love and trust rather than fear and doubt.

- Knowing that today is the first day of the rest of your life, how shall you enter it? If you remember the words of John Wayne, you'll enter it with a clean heart and an open mind because yesterday ended at midnight. With this in mind, every morning when you swing your feet out of bed, the portal to a (re)defining moment is right there waiting for you to step through it. That is the power of forgiveness.

As a Mindfulness Practice, Consider the Following:

As a way to embody the concepts presented in this chapter, consider doing the following steps daily for the next thirty days and witness how it changes your perception of life and the accessibility to the presence of the true Self.

Part 1

To determine if you are complete in your forgiveness practice, begin with this self-inquiry process:

1. Think of the person(s) or incident(s) you believe you have forgiven, and do a quick scan of your emotions, sitting with them for a moments.
2. Is there any residue of resentment lingering in your mind and heart as you hold an image of that person(s) or

incident(s)? A good way to tell is by listening to your body, not just your mind. What does your physical body report? Listen closely, because it will never lie, even if your mind wants to convince you otherwise.

3. Does the memory drag you out of the present moment and into the past, where you relive the experience, negative emotions playing in an endless loop, or are you able to objectively be the observer of the event without being drawn back into it? If you find you are complete with your forgiveness, you may go directly to #8. If you are still incomplete with your forgiveness, continue this process.

Part 2

If you felt resistance or energy move in an uncomfortable way while exploring the above questions, proceed below:

4. The practice is to remember that a memory is just a thought until you assign a meaning or attach a feeling to it. It may help to remember you are no more your feelings than you are your body. Your feelings are simply energy impulses moving through the body that tell you what is going on in your mind.

5. Understand that severing the emotional tie to a past negative experience does not in any way discount the experience—it sets you free from being a victim of it in the future.

6. Forgiving doesn't mean you are condoning the actions that evoked your resentment. It means you are willing to set

yourself free by not "resending" future toxins of resentment elicited by the event through your mind and body,
again and again.

7. Remember, forgiveness doesn't necessarily mean forgetting. We may always have memories attached to some of
our emotional wounds in much the same way we have scar
tissue from a physical wound that happened long ago. That
doesn't mean you have to relive the pain that caused the
scar.

8. To conclude this exercise, take a deep, intentional, cleansing breath; take the vertical plunge to your center; and
experience the Life Force present there. Allow yourself to
be bathed in the Light that has been there since the first
day you slipped into your earth suit. Your wound is simply
the opening through which you are now being guided
back to the true Self. Welcome home.

CHAPTER 13

The One Thing
We All Have in Common

There Is Really Only One of Us Here

Within man is the soul of the whole; the wise silence; the universal beauty, to which every part and particle is equally related; the eternal ONE. And this deep power in which we exist and whose beatitude is all accessible to us, is not only self-sufficing and perfect in every hour, but the act of seeing and the thing seen, the seer and the spectacle, the subject and the object, are one. We see the world piece by piece, as the sun, the moon, the animal, the tree; but the whole of which these things are the shining parts, is the soul.

—RALPH WALDO EMERSON

Earlier in this book, I spoke about the difference between *what* we are and *who* we are. Ralph Waldo Emerson referred to the Original Self (the *what*) as the eternal One or the Oversoul. The blending of the *what* and the *who* is the ultimate paradox described in the classic metaphor of the ocean. The question is, are you the ocean or the drop of water that momentarily seems to separate from the ocean as a wave crashes on the rocks, sending a spray of what appears to be individual drops of water skyward only to, at some point, fall back into the ocean? The answer is yes; we are both the ocean and the drop of ocean water because even in the apparent state of separation, all the inherent qualities of the whole are contained in the part. Using the ocean as metaphor, there is only one of us here—we all share the same intrinsic qualities because we originate from the same source. But as the drop of water, we take on our own unique, albeit temporary, form of expression only to, at some point, merge again with the source from which we came. As Margaret Mead put it, "Always remember that you are absolutely unique. Just like everyone else."

The question is, although we understand there is only one *what* from which we have all come, have you given much thought to why there are so many individual *who*'s on the planet? Just as the mystics knew, when the quest to understand the relationship between what you are and who you are becomes your desire, your (re)defining moments will be lined up like the lights on an airport landing strip, sequentially guiding you back to your authentic self and, in the process, you'll discover the crucial role that authentic relationships play in that process. In a manner of speaking, your conscious and authentic relationships are the lights on the runway that assist you in remembering the way home.

Conscious Relationships Matter

"Interactions with parents, and with those whom you have chosen to share your intimacy, and with those with whom— out of the billions of souls on our planet—you share parts of your life, serve to activate within you an awareness of who you are and what you are here to do . . . Open yourself

to your fellow humans . . . It is not until you have the courage
to engage in human relationships that you grow."
—GARY ZUKAV, *The Seat of the Soul*

Life is a trip we were not meant to travel alone. If we stop and
consider our life, we shall see that we entered into a lifetime of
relationships beginning the moment we arrived. From our birth
mother, followed by other family members, and literally every
other person we have met along the journey, this thing called
life has been interwoven like a string of fine pearls on one single
invisible silver thread called relationships. It is the authentic relationships we create along the way that help shape and beautify
our lives by the mere reflection of the light of all those encounters. Often it is in the process of creating authentic relationships
that some of our most profound (re)defining moments arise. In
those moments, we intuitively know when we have connected
with a fellow traveler on the pilgrimage leading back to the
Original Self.

When the topic of relationships comes up, the tendency for
most of us is to immediately think "significant other" relationships because it seems that is where we invest a majority of our
time. However, when we pause and consider the many other
people with whom we connect on a daily basis, we'll see that
our lives are filled with relationships on numerous different levels. For me, the realization is that without all of them, life would
be meaningless. From the strangers I chat with while out and
about doing various errands, to my most beloved family members (including my dog, Mac) and everyone in between, without
them, I would not want to be here. Without those relationships,
life would be hollow. While life itself is the ultimate gift from
the Creator, relationships are how the gift is woven into the tap-

estry of a life worth living. Each separate thread, when combined with the others, adds a color, richness, and dimension to life that we could never experience without them.

This desire for connection has become even more evident with the increased popularity of social media, especially Facebook and Twitter. It has become quite obvious that, at the end of the day, what people are seeking is connection—where they inherently know that their lives are enriched by sharing them with others. The practice is to value your relationships, treasure your friendships, and don't take them for granted, because each one is a rich reminder of how blessed you are. Your friendships truly represent, to a large extent, the tapestry of your life. The reality is that unless we live isolated and alone at the top of a mountain, having relationships is not an option; from the moment our feet hit the floor in the morning, we enter into a continuum of encounters, beginning with the face we see staring back at us in the mirror. So it's not a matter of "if" we will have relationships; it's a question of "how conscious" we shall be in them. How mindfully awake we are will determine what we bring and receive from them and the depth of authenticity in which we do so.

The poet and artist Flavia made a profound statement about relationships when he wrote, "Some people come into our lives and quickly go. Some people stay for a while, and give us a deeper understanding of what is truly important in this life. They touch our souls . . . we gain strength from the footprints they have left on our heart and we will never be the same." In other words, every relationship we have, from our significant others, family, and friends, to our neighbors and coworkers, and even the occasional stranger we allow into our lives, all bear something in common. Each will leave "footprints" on our heart, as we will on theirs. Those footprints may leave a positive or negative impression, but in either case, each relationship brings with it—if we are conscious—an opportunity to learn more about our authentic self and the role each person plays in shaping *who* it is we have come to this planet to be. Through either pain or pleasure, joy or sorrow, relationships open the portal to more (re)defining moments than any other single thing because, *if we are conscious*, they lead the mind to the heart, where the truth of who we are lies in silent repose. Suffice it to say, our relationships are a super highway to the heart.

Don't Confuse Intimacy with Authenticity

"Enlightenment is the key to everything, and it is the key to intimacy, because it is the goal of true authenticity."
—MARIANNE WILLIAMSON

Enlightenment is looking beyond all conditions in the human realm and seeing only infinite Presence. It allows us the ability to see the light within ourselves and others—to see the deeper truth of who we all are. As such, enlightenment can be thought of as the connective tissue between intimacy and authenticity— and there is a need for both—but we must not to confuse one for the other. All our relationships have much in common. Many of the same principles that apply to the relationship we have with those closest to us also apply to those farther from the hub of our lives—the only differentiating factor is the degree of intimacy we shall allow between them. The problem occurs when we confuse intimacy with authenticity. Although the term *Into-Me-See* has been floating around for so many years it has become a New Age parody of the word *intimacy,* it is still quite an accurate way of describing how far we are willing to allow others to see into us, to know us.

Imagine a series of concentric circles drawn around each other, from a small circle to a much larger one, such as you might see as an archer's target. At the center of the circle are the relationships you have with those closest to you—the ones with whom you are likely to be more "intimate," meaning those whom you allow to "see into you" more fully because you feel safe with them. As the circles expand outward, the relationships are less and less intimate and, therefore, your tendency may be to reveal less and less of yourself. As an example: at the center of your hub may be your partner, then a bit farther out a family member, then even farther out a relative, then even farther out a neighbor, then a coworker, then the clerk at the grocery store, then a stranger on an airplane, and so on. These varying degrees of intimacy are appropriate, but don't confuse intimacy with your need to be *equally* authentic with every human being—be they family, friends, or strangers. In other words, not that you would or should desire the same depth of intimacy with every person with whom you have contact, but you must be totally authentic in *every* relationship you have—holding nothing back. Can you imagine the (re)defining moments that would be born from being that present with others? Being conscious in all our relationships is a high calling.

Conscious Relationships Lay the Foundation for Authentic Relationships

The more conscious and spiritually grounded we are in our relationships, the more authentic they become.

Is it possible to have authentic relationships wherein we can be who we truly are and, at the same time, create space for others to be who they truly are? I propose that it is not only possible, but it will become the norm for any person who is willing to make the commitment to do the work. Authenticity is the passageway leading directly to the soul, and our "relation-ships" can be the sacred vessels we board to explore this passageway. Our relation-ships are the vehicles for our own personal evolution as individuals and a species. If we are conscious, our relationships offer us the clearest view of our own soul because they invite us to look directly into the face of another and see, not only our own reflection but also the face of the Divine. From a spiritual perspective, we have come here to have relationships. From the cradle to the grave and all along the way in between, it is the relationships we have on the journey that truly make life worth living, so why not make the journey consciously and with authenticity?

> "Each of us is here for a brief sojourn; for what purpose he knows not, though he senses it. But without deeper reflection one knows from daily life that one exists for other people."
> —ALBERT EINSTEIN

Every person desires relationship—someone to witness their life—to reflect to them the truth of who they are and that who they are matters. From this perspective, Einstein is spot-on; we truly do exist for one another's sake. This is the spiritual component that drives our deep desire for connection with other human beings, even if we are not consciously aware of it. The paradox is, out of the One, the many are manifest and drawn together to remind ourselves that we are not alone—that individually and collectively, we are part of something far greater than ourselves.

Looking into the Heart of the Matter

"You must look into people, as well as at them."
—Lord Chesterfield

When you are in conversation, face-to-face with another person, how engaged are you in authentic communication? There is a profound difference between talking *with* someone and talking *at* them. As you enter into conscious communication, you'll notice you go to a deeper place; your mind is present and not running out in front of the conversation, thinking about what you are going to say next or wondering where you'll be going for lunch. When mindfully present and engaged in the moment, your mind will connect you to your heart—and when you speak from your heart directly to the heart of another, you are communicating authentically. This is when the true you recognizes itself in another.

Conscious and authentic relationships draw upon their oneness, not only to sustain themselves but to evolve themselves. When we live in the deep awareness of our oneness with life, the authentic self within begins to unfold and recognize itself in others. This is when we naturally begin to treat one another with reverence, compassion, and loving-kindness. The key is to find a practice that helps us remember the truth of who we are and "why" we are. In various parts of Asia and beyond, when the word *Namaste* (which is derived from the ancient language of Sanskrit) is spoken to another person, it is an acknowledgment, a conscious practice, of this truth. While there are variations of the literal meaning of the word *Namaste,* I favor the definition given by Mahatma Gandhi: "I honor the place within you where the entire Universe resides; I honor the place within you of Love, of Light, of Truth, of Peace; I honor the place within you where, when you are in that place in you, and I am in that place in me, there is only one of us."

What more needs to be said other than *Namaste*? Any other words just seem to get in the way.

Why We Seek Relationships

"We are each driven by a deep urge to form an intimate connection with the world around us and most of us do this through relationships. If you take a soul look at this, you will see that your need for relationship actually stems from your basic human need to overcome your earthly sense of separation."

—CAROLINE REYNOLDS, *Spiritual Fitness*

Baseball legend Ty Cobb said, "If I had the chance to live my life over, I'd do things a little different . . . I'd have more friends." His wisdom is sage: I don't want to wait until the end of my life to understand the importance and meaning of having shared my life with true friends; it's the journey we take together that matters most, not the destination. What I know is that every new friendship offers us another opportunity to build a bridge to a person's heart and soul, which, in turn, reminds us that we are never alone as long as the bridge is maintained. Perhaps even more important, with every authentic friendship comes the opportunity to witness the greatness of who that person really is and, in the process, be reminded that we wouldn't be able to see it in them if it didn't also live within us.

Knowing we are all emanations of the Original Self, some

say the Universe is quite the trickster, doing it all with mirrors, and yet, if you were to look closely at the seven billion "mirrors" currently occupying the planet, not one of us reflect exactly the same image. Why is this? Spiritually speaking, there is no need for two of anything exactly the same because it would be redundant; while the Universe loves multiplicity and is infinitely prolific in individuated forms of expression, each one is unique and unlike any other. This is why striving to live from your authentic self is so important; it honors the purpose you are here to serve—*to be you*—and no one else can "do you" better than you. This is equally important to remember when your life path intersects with other "personalities" by means of those interesting encounters we call relationships. Honoring other people's need to be uniquely who they are, rather than who we think they should be, is to honor the Divine intention imbued in them as they, too, arrived on the planet to be a one-of-a-kind emanation of Light and matter tightly consolidated into a space suit called a body.

We All Share the Same Name

"Not Christian or Jew, Muslim, not Hindu, Buddhist, Sufi, Zen. Not any religion or culture system. I am not from the East or the West, not out of the ocean or up from the ground, not natural or ethereal, not composed of elements at all . . . I belong to the Beloved, have seen the two worlds as One and that One call to know, first, last, outer, inner, only that breath breathing Human Being."

—RUMI

When I think about the countless "mirrors" who currently occupy the planet, reflecting the One, and the difference even one of those mirrors can make in setting the stage for a (re)defining moment in another person's life, my memory takes me back to a life-changing experience I had in China while leading a sacred journey excursion in 2007. Years later, my mind is still processing what my eyes witnessed and heart experienced in a land and culture that is so profoundly different from what I could have ever imagined. From the beginning, with a total of thirty-eight sojourners in our group, "The Ancient Wisdom" tour took on a life of its own. Upon arrival in Beijing, we hit the ground running and never stopped. Our group seemed to move with a singular sense of elegance, grace, and flow that very much reflected the energy of the culture in which we were immersed. Each historical landmark and ancient structure we visited seemed to top the one before in its immensity of scale, detail, and beauty. Every experience of contemporary China added a new depth of appreciation for a culture that has adapted amazingly fast to westernization while still maintaining its ancient roots.

Each new day I kept anxiously waiting for my "next" experience of China, assuming it couldn't possibly be greater than the last. I mean, what could possibly be greater than standing on the Great Wall itself, or more stunning and breathtaking than a mindfulness walk through the Forbidden City? Then, one day during lunch, at a small local (nontourist) restaurant in downtown Beijing that Yin, our guide, referred to as "The Shouting Restaurant," it happened. My peak experience for the entire journey divinely exploded before my eyes. The name of the restaurant was appropriate enough; with everyone conversing at the top of their lungs while different courses of food were being served in rapid-fire order, the energy was absolutely magnetic. No, my epiphany didn't happen while drinking the dead-snake-in-the-bottle wine or eating a fiery, spice-soaked dumpling; it was in the eyes of a small child, perhaps three or four years of age, who stood motionless outside the restaurant peering directly through the window into my eyes.

In that magical moment, time stood still. I could see her mind at work, thinking about me . . . as if she recognized me and was trying to remember if and how she knew me. Then suddenly, as if she realized I was a member of her own family, her eyes lit up even more, she giggled and cracked a big smile that bridged any possibility of a chasm between cultures, age, and language, dissolving all barriers between us. In that pristine moment, she and I truly did know one another. We had connected with something we both inherently had in common— our humanity, as well as our oneness in something infinitely larger than life itself; at peak moments such as this the veil between the two is very thin. When we can look beyond size, age, gender, nationality, color, culture, religion, or any of the other many labels we tend to place upon others and ourselves, we realize we are all very much the same. We all are born; we all die. We all laugh; we all cry. We all know joy; we all know pain. We all share the same planet, and we all share the same name: Human Being. Again, it is through our commonality that we find our uniqueness as well—and all it takes is a simple gaze into another's eyes while we remember that *who* we are looking at is actually a reflection of some aspect of ourselves . . . followed, of course, by the universal language of a smile to bridge any perceived communication gap.

Only after having this peak moment did I look up, at first somewhat startled, to see the child's mother standing there grinning from ear to ear. She no doubt took great pleasure in witnessing her daughter's delight in our encounter. Clearly this child had a great role model for openness to others, who, at first glance, may appear "different." About that time, everyone sitting at my table got in on the action and began smiling and waving to this beautiful child and her proud mom, who both replied with more of the same. It was one of those profound moments that will be indelibly etched into the walls of my mind and heart forever.

So there I was, 7,000 miles away from home, fully expecting to experience my divine ah-ha moment while standing next to the Grand Canal in Suzhou, doing Tai Chi with hundreds of others at the Temple of Heaven in Beijing, being mesmerized in the presence of the Terracotta Warriors, while sitting in silent prayer at the Wild Goose Pagoda in Xian, or gazing at the stunning nighttime skyline of skyscrapers along the Bund in Shanghai. No. All it took was one small child who was willing to allow me to see myself, my soul, and all of humanity in her. This was, without question, a (re)defining moment for me because it opened my heart and mind to the possibilities of a world that works for everyone based on a deepened awareness that, regardless of our ethnicity, culture, color, politics, age, gender, or size, we are all beautiful and unique drops of the Beloved One dancing freely with one another in an Infinite Ocean of Sameness.

I returned home from that amazing trip humbled and reminded that, at the end of the day, life is really about relationships. If we are willing to look deeply enough *into* one another, getting past all of our judgments and fears about our differences, we will be able to see what we have in common. In short, we'll remember to remember there is only One of us here. Contained within the wisdom of this awareness lies the potential for a lasting peace in our world. How could we possibly conspire to do harm to another when we see ourselves in them? Do you need to go 7,000 miles to be reminded of this? Of course not. You need look no farther than the next person you encounter today.

The Sufi mystic Rumi summarized it beautifully when he wrote, "In any gathering, in any chance meeting on the street, there is a shine, an elegance rising up." May this be the day you rise up and meet and greet your true Self in another; it could be the portal to a (re)defining moment for you and them. Just let the light of your authentic self shine, and go where it leads you.

POINTS TO PONDER AND PERSONALIZE

- Considering the metaphor of the ocean and the drop of water that momentarily separates itself from the ocean, can you see yourself as both? Is this not an empowering realization?

- Can you see the paradox in Margaret Mead's words, "Always remember that you are absolutely unique. Just like everyone else"? Every human being is animated by the *same* Life Force, and yet each one is unique in how they express the life they have been given. Can you honor the uniqueness in you as well as all other beings?

- When you think of "relationships," who do you include in that circle, and who might you exclude? Have you ever considered that, at some level, you are having a relationship with every person who enters your circle—from the most outer circumference to the absolute center of your circle? The question is, how conscious will you be in *all* of them—how much of your authentic self are you bringing to all of them?

- Intimacy and authenticity are two important aspects of relationships. Can you see how intimacy determines the degree of familiarity you have in your relationships while authenticity determines the manner in which you bring the true you *equally* into all of them? Living from your authentic self never excludes anyone.

- How far does the idea resonate that every relationship you have, at some level, reflects the relationship you are having with yourself? If you find yourself recoiling at that suggestion, you may want to give it some thought. If you are mindful, this could be an opening to a major (re)defining moment in your life. As you refocus your perception of yourself, you'll begin to see others differently as well. When you begin to seek and find the oneness you share with others, you'll also discover you have more in common rather than differences.

As a Mindfulness Practice, Consider the Following:

1. When you take the time to look into another person rather than just at them, what do you see? Just sit with this question for a moment. It is an important self-inquiry process to perform before doing the following exercise.

2. The next person you have a face-to-face conversation with, make a conscious effort to look into their eyes, re-

gardless of whether you are speaking or listening. Connect with your breath, and consciously slow down your breathing while focusing solely on the words being spoken, irrespective of who is speaking them. Remember that words are but symbols of what is passing through the mind and heart.

3. Listen with your ears and heart, and when you speak, do so mindfully and with reverence in your voice and heart, reflecting the sacredness of the being in front of you.

4. Finally, realize that, whether it is the barista at your local coffee shop, the teller at the bank, your beloved partner, or your cherished child, you are surrounded by beautiful mirrors reflecting to you. In other words, when done mindfully, every person who stands before you offers you an opportunity to look directly into the eyes of the One and witness It seeing Itself in you. I would encourage you to not just look at the people in your experience today, but to look into them and silently say, "Namaste."

Note: If you are currently on Facebook and we have not yet connected, let's do so. The journey is far too good not to share it with like-minded souls! I would be honored to add you to the tapestry of my life. <https://www.facebook.com/DennisMerrittJones> I also invite you to follow me on Twitter @DMerrittJones.

CHAPTER 14

Staying Teachable: The Touchstone to Endless (Re)Defining Moments

The Wisdom in Knowing There Is More to Know

Here is the test to find whether your mission on Earth is fin-ished: if you're alive, it isn't.

—RICHARD BACH, *Illusions*

There is some good news and some other news about the pilgrimage back to where living an authentic life begins. I purposefully chose not to mention this at the beginning of our journey together because I didn't want it to be an impediment to actualizing the unique, authentic being you were born to be. The good news is, if you are mindfully committed to practicing the ideas presented in this book, you will, if you haven't already, arrive at a place where living an authentic life comes as natural and effortless to you as taking your next breath. It will be obvi-ous when you have reached this point because your life will take on an entirely different hue and dimension—you'll see yourself and your world through new eyes. The "other" news, however, is that this is not the end of your journey. Just because you have arrived at a point where authentic living is the norm doesn't mean there is no room to go deeper.

The inherent risk in finding your way back to your ancient roots and connecting to the Original Self lies in the mistaken belief that once you have "arrived," your journey is complete and there is nothing more to do, no new depths to plumb. Sorry to say, nothing could be further from the truth. While you may indeed experience the satisfaction of having made the hero's journey, having nowhere else to go is not an option. Despite *who* you may think you are, as long as you live in a human skin, there will always be new dimensions of your authentic self to explore and integrate into your world. Think of it this way: whether you are a "butcher, baker, or candlestick maker" and are considered the best at what you "do," there was an entry point at which you started where you were forced into a learning curve, and you did it. You leaned into what you didn't yet know and grew. You went deeper into your inherent ability to expand your base of knowledge with a sense of faith that what you needed to know you would learn and you did . . . and that process has never ended. That is because you stayed teachable. Likewise, by continuing to plumb the eternal depths of what lies below the surface of what you "do," you'll discover there will always be more to know about who and what you truly "are." That is because *what* you are is an individuated spark of an infinite Light, and there is no edge where It ceases to be. Given this understanding, can you see how "becoming" who you were born to be is a pilgrimage back to the One from which you came?

Until the day you lay aside your earth suit of flesh and bones and your soul returns to the essence from which it came, an ocean of infinite possibilities called life is yours to fathom. Your soul is hardwired for this mission—which, as I have stated throughout this book, is, in part, to explore *unknown* territory and gather new soul-expanding information through direct experience. Clearly there is a lot of unknown territory lying just outside the realm of your current consciousness. From the moment you recognize who you truly are, every day will offer you yet another opportunity to reinvent yourself, to (re)define yourself. It is in this context that I say there is great wisdom in knowing there will always be more to know; staying teachable is a lifetime practice that lifts you beyond the danger of ever thinking you have arrived at a point of completion. As Richard Bach infers, if you are still an occupant on the planet, there is more for you to do—especially once you can do it as a fully conscious, authentic being. The world needs more human beings who are grounded in authenticity—people who comprehend who they truly are. Consider that your "life lessons," be they wonderful or less than wonderful, are the Universe's way of directing you back to your authentic self. In other words, despite how evolved you consider yourself to be, as long as you occupy a human body, there will be more to know about "you." With this in mind, let us deepen our understanding of what "staying teachable" means.

Staying Teachable Is the Pathway of Awakened Wisdom

"Wisdom comes from experience.
Experience is often a result of lack of wisdom."
—TERRY PRATCHETT

The aforementioned quote is reminiscent of the classic conundrum found in the question, "What comes first, the chicken or the egg?" but it is, nonetheless, an accurate statement. Our toughest life experiences can dig the well from which we draw our deepest wisdom if we are conscious enough to learn from those experiences. Staying teachable is the practice we must master for a lifetime. If we are open and willing to learn from our past—be it good or not so good—we can use it in a manner that guarantees a deeper understanding of our soul's mission to evolve itself. Even after we achieve the goal of living an authentic life, staying teachable assures us that there are yet many more (re)defining moments ahead that will forever alter our lives in yet unimagined ways. The questions might arise, "But how many times can, or must, we (re)define ourselves? How much more of the truth about ourselves can we know beyond the fact that we are one with an expanding Universe—an Infinite Intelligence that has individuated Itself, in part, as you and me?" The answers are contained within the questions: as long as we live in a body that occupies space on this planet, we will be given endless opportunities to dive more deeply into the infinite bottomless ocean of Divinity from which we came. Knowing how and when to draw upon our wisdom is the diving board that will lift us to a new perspective of life and who we really are and then plunge us deeper into the infinite depths of the Original Self.

Having Wisdom and Knowing How to Use It Are Two Different Things

Knowledge gained *and remembered* can point the way to a (re)defining moment. When Albert Einstein defined insanity as doing

the same thing over and over again and expecting different results, I suspect he was drawing on the knowledge he gained from
years of experiments, including those that worked and—perhaps
more so—those that failed. Few would disagree that Einstein
was a wise man. If a bona fide genius understood the value of
drawing upon his acquired wisdom to maintain his place in the
creative flow of an expanding, evolving Universe, perhaps there
is something here for us to learn as well. What is wisdom, really?
Wisdom is a collection of our past "learning" experiences lodged
in our memory bank, *remembered* and drawn upon when needed,
and then applied to the issue in the present moment in a manner
that affects a desired outcome in the future. If you know anyone
who has repeatedly relived the same painful experience again
and again, it is because they failed to deposit the experience in
their memory bank (their wisdom well) and apply learned lessons to the current circumstance. Perhaps this is why our elders
are considered wiser than young people; they have had more
time to make multiple deposits in their personal acquired wisdom well.

Don't mistake this form of remembering prior experiences
with being resentfully stuck in the past (our hi-story) and not
living in the present moment. As we discovered in chapter 12 on
forgiveness, when we have consciously discharged any negative
emotions wrapped around a specific memory, it becomes nothing more than a thought that is adding a solid bit of wisdom to
the well. The practice is to be mindful enough of your experiences today that, when applicable, the appropriate ones can be
deposited in your wisdom well for future reference (after de-
toxifying them of anger and resentment). A wise person does not
forget their past experiences; they remember them clearly, but
for the *right reasons*—to apply them in the present moment in a

manner that creates a better outcome tomorrow. The deeper we can dive into our own wisdom well, the closer we are drawn to the genius of the authentic self. As Einstein did, if you are mindful and willing to learn from your less-than-rewarding experiences today, you can draw deeply from your wisdom well in the future and avoid the pain of reliving the same experience and outcome over and over again. You don't really have to be a genius to know this, but, as you'll see below, sometimes we all need a little help remembering.

How Often Do You Have to Repeat the Same Mistake?

"A learning experience is one of those things that says, 'You know that thing you just did? Don't do that.'"
—Douglas Adams

Living in the foothills of Southern California, we have an abundance of rattlesnakes—several of which have previously visited my backyard. This motivated me to take my dog, MacDoodle, to a Rattlesnake Avoidance class in which live rattlesnakes are used to give the dogs a real-time "learning experience" they, hopefully, do not soon forget. With the snakes safely and humanely muzzled (how they do that I'll never know—nor do I want to know), the trainer placed an electric shock collar on Mac and then led him to the first snake. Mac, being the curious critter he is, moved as close as he possibly could to the rattler for an up-close and personal experience of what "snake" is. When he was within striking distance of the snake, the trainer delivered a mild electrical impulse to Mac's collar (which I first experienced and found to be more startling than painful). Mac was immediately given a lesson that was etched in his young puppy mind: "rattlesnake" equates to a certain degree of unpleasantness.

While he probably didn't see it as such, you could say it was a (re)defining moment for him because it altered Mac's level of awareness about being in the moment and paying attention to the growth opportunity that could affect his future in a beneficent manner. It took two more "learning experiences" with different snakes, and he was a believer. The third time the trainer tried to bring him near a snake, Mac wanted nothing to do with it. He really got the essence of Douglas Adams's aforementioned quote, "You know that thing you just did? Don't do that." And here is the most salient point: this only happened because the trainer kept Mac *present and engaged* with the experience until he learned the lesson. That is the way it is with (re)defining moments—we have to be present and engaged in the moment because that is where the opening to a greater awareness and our oneness with life is waiting to get our attention.

How about you? Do you ever have challenges staying engaged with your "life-learning lessons"? Have you noticed that there is a direct correlation between how many times you tend to repeatedly make the same mistake and the degree of unpleasantness or pain you experience as a consequence of making that mistake? The more pain involved, the fewer times you tend to make the same mistake—or at least in theory, that is how it is supposed to work. The problem with this theory is that, although it may work well for dogs wearing shock collars, humans seem more difficult to train. The theory doesn't take into account the gravitational pull of denial and instant gratification to which humans are so susceptible. Too often we avoid, deny, or numb the pain rather than allowing it be our teacher. It seems many people will do just about anything to avoid dealing with not only the pain, but also the linear process of embodying the lesson (meaning depositing it in the wisdom well to be drawn upon later). Embodying the lesson buried in the pain can only be accomplished by remaining mindfully connected to the moment and staying with the experience rather than running from it. Like the dog, the more quickly we get the message and learn the lesson, the less unpleasantness and pain we will be subjected to.

You Can Run but You Can't Hide from a Lesson with Your Name on It

"Wherever you go, there you are."

—JON KABAT-ZINN

Whether we know it or not, when we fail to lean in and embrace the lesson being offered, we are sending a signal to the Universe that essentially says, "Hey . . . I want more of the same." The law of attraction will never fail in drawing to us whatever reflects our predominant thoughts and deepest beliefs. As an example, many of us have gone from one disastrous relationship or unsatisfactory job to the next, and then the next, ad infinitum, never stopping long enough to explore the possibility that each failed experience had something to teach us. You can run but you can't hide from yourself. While the next person's name and hair color may change, the "issues" don't. While the next job may appear to have different coworkers, amazingly enough, the same "problem" people show up in different bodies.

We can't outrun our self-limiting behaviors and beliefs because they will follow us like our own shadow; however, we can transcend them by exposing them to the light of present-moment awareness. The practice is to pay attention to what is going on in the moment and learn what it has to teach us. The payoff is that a consistent mind-set of knowing there is more to know in every sacred moment is like priming the pump for a (re)defining moment long before we see it coming. As mentioned in chapter 1, the key is to remember that any and every moment holds the potential to be a (re)defining opportunity because, contained within it, there is the possibility to be changed by what it brings—*if* we are conscious, aware, and willing to embrace it. We simply need to be mindful when they pop up. As uncomfortable as it may be sometimes, if we are mindful and willing to look deeply enough *into* a (re)defining moment when it presents itself, we'll see the authentic self right there, trying to get our attention, trying to remind us who we really are. This is the reward to be found in remaining teachable; an opportunity to change our mind, our behavior, and, ultimately, our life.

While Mac's motivation to change his behavior was stimulated by the unpleasant impulse of a shock collar, at the end of the day, the learned response from the shock (in that moment) may save him from much worse pain and suffering in the future. That is called "delayed gratification." What lesson is life trying to teach you today about repeatedly re-creating the same unpleasant experiences? You never know—there could be a (re)defining moment just waiting for you, buried in the midst of the discomfort. Odd as it seems, that is the purpose of pain—to get your attention, to open you to knowing that there is more to know about yourself and what you are doing here. Hey, if a dog can learn the meaning of "You know that thing you just did? Don't do that," there is hope for you and me. The lesson from my teacher Mac is that life doesn't have to be so "ruff"—we just need to be present and teachable in the moment . . . and what better time to start than right now? Consider yourself buzzed.

Every Experience Nourishes You If You Let It

> "One of the shining qualities that heroes possess is the willingness to be educated by all things. They learn from the most impressive variety of people and experiences: the wise and the foolish; the obvious and the inconceivable; the living and the dead; the things they love and the things they hate . . . 'Everything nourished him,' Henry Miller once said of Goethe."
>
> —GREGG LEVOY, *Callings*

What Gregg Levoy refers to as a hero, I would refer to as an awakened, evolving person on a quest to grow and better understand life and their relationship with it. This type of hero is rare because they have the willingness to stand toe-to-toe with "what is," to explore it and ultimately become a better person because of the encounter. Have you ever considered that everyone and everything that stands before you in every given moment of your life is an invitation from the Universe to learn something vitally important to your own continuing education, evolution, and growth? Is it really possible that you could be "nourished" by *every* experience you have, be it positive or negative? It's easy to imagine good things coming from that which we consider pleasant, but the objectionable things require us to dig much deeper into the experience to find the value in them.

Having a willingness to be educated by *all* things is a tall (perhaps heroic) order, but consider the benefits: if you can remain teachable, every person, circumstance, and event in your life gives you the opportunity to live more fully from your authentic self—to grow stronger and wiser—if you are willing to receive the lesson.

> "A disciple . . . can never imitate his guide's steps. You have your own way of living your life, of dealing with problems, and of winning. Teaching is only demonstrating that it is possible. Learning is making it possible for yourself."
> —PAULO COELHO, *The Pilgrimage*

As discussed in chapter 2, I am an ardent believer in the universal imperative, "Grow or die." Essentially, what this means is that living things that cease growing begin to die; their Life Force slowly withdraws, and they begin to wither, ultimately returning to the ethers from which they came. This not only includes the potted plant growing in our kitchen bay window, it includes us. When we cease growing, we begin dying. By being open to the "experience" being offered in the daily school of life, we receive the stimulus to encourage our ongoing growth in the same manner a root-bound plant does when it is transplanted in a larger pot. The vital thing to remember is that regardless of how young or old we are, when we cease growing, we are literally sending a message to the Universe that says, "I am finished here. . . . There is no point in me hanging around any longer, so bring me home." Staying teachable is like repotting ourselves in a larger growing environment when we think we have arrived at a point of completion and have nothing more to learn about who we really are. The practice is to stay dialed into the fact that we are just infants on a universal learning curve and to remain engaged in knowing there is more to know about ourselves and the Universe with which we are one.

Making Space to Receive the Teaching

> "The Universe is one great kindergarten for man. Everything that exists has brought with it its own peculiar lesson. The mountain teaches stability and grandeur; the ocean immensity and change. Forests, lakes, and rivers, clouds and winds, stars and flowers, stupendous glaciers and crystal snowflakes—every form of animate or inanimate existence, leaves its impress upon the soul of man."
>
> —ORISON SWETT MARDEN

What does it require to be open to receiving the impress or experience that life continually offers to us? First, it requires the willingness to see everyone and everything as a source of new information and inspiration—a stimulus that will support us in our own evolution and expansion. Second, we must develop a grateful heart for the lessons offered. Khalil Gibran wrote, "I have learnt silence from the talkative, toleration from the intolerant, and kindness from the unkind; yet strange, I am ungrateful to these teachers." The essence of his message is that too often we fail to be aware of the value of having such individuals and experiences in our lives because we are so busy reacting, judging, or avoiding them, there is no space or time to receive their teaching. Gratitude softens and opens our heart to receive the gift. The added bonus is that often that gift comes in the form of a (re)defining moment in which we are given the opportunity to see the soul being we really are reflected in the eyes of another, or in simply realizing our oneness with life in that moment.

Staying Teachable Means Not Taking Things Personal

> "The Universe always strikes you at your weakest point because that's what most needs strengthening."
>   —JOSEPH CAMPBELL

I don't like the idea that the Universe "strikes" anyone, but I do believe there is great wisdom in Joseph Campbell's words when we see the lesson in the metaphor: the Universe continually conspires for our good, even when it may not feel good. How can this be? The Universe, while infinite and intelligent, operates by means of the law of cause and effect. Regardless of whether we know it or not, we work with the law of cause and effect by means of our consciousness (belief system), which, in turn, activates the law of attraction, drawing to us precisely what we have embodied as the truth about ourselves and life in general. My point is, it is difficult to receive the lessons being offered to us by the Universe if we take personally the consequences yielded by our ignorance of and misuse of an impersonal law. What part of our belief system needs strengthening? It is really quite easy to deduce because the answer is to be found, as Campbell infers, where we are demonstrating the greatest challenges—where we appear to be the weakest. If there were ever a precedent set for a (re)defining moment, this would be it—if we would open to "what is" and invite the teacher within to help us see it as such. These are the moments when the pain can crack us open so we may see more deeply into the truth of who we authentically are at the center of our being.

The key is to remember, in those moments when we feel the most vulnerable and challenged by less-than-fortuitous circumstances, to stay teachable—to know that we are at choice. We can think of ourselves as either helpless victims of a cruel, capricious, and merciless Universe, or students in "Earth School" (a term coined by author Gary Zukav) on a *conscious* quest to grow stronger, wiser, and more compassionate by means of the vertical path that takes us higher and, at the same time, deeper into our center. When we are teachable, we'll see that strength is gained by taking action in a proactive way that moves us forward.

Awareness is knowing when to make a withdrawal from our wisdom well. Compassion is what we extend to others who bear the personal scars of their journey through the valley of vulnerability. We can all use a cheerleader at those times when we feel the weakest. The practice is to be conscious enough to see our weak points as the gateway to greatness, rather than defeat, remembering that the Universe is always on our side even if, in the moment, it may not feel that way. The tree blesses the harshest wind that causes its roots to grow deeper and, thus, stronger. Bless your weakest points; it's not what the Universe dishes out to you that forms your character, it's how you choose to use it to your advantage in a manner that enables you to grow with grace and ease into the amazing, creative expression of Life you have come here to be. In staying teachable, you ensure your own unique place in a Universe that delights in pushing out, even beyond the realm of Its own farthest Light.

Points to Ponder and Personalize

• How does it feel to know that even after your sojourn back to your authentic self has been reached, it is really not a point of arrival so much as it is a new point of departure to an even deeper knowing of who you are? Being aware of how you truly feel about this concept is the mark of a wise person.

• Since antiquity, wise men and women have declared, "The moment you arrive at a point where you believe you have nothing more to know, the reality is you know nothing at all." To actualize the truth of this statement is to open yourself to a (re)defining moment. As long as you live in a human skin, evolving itself is your soul's divine assignment, and there is no area of your life where that concept is excluded. Remaining teachable is a statement to the Universe that you know there is more to know and, therefore, more for you to grow.

• Can you see how being teachable is a sure way to make regular deposits in your wisdom well? Staying teachable allows you to remain engaged in the present moment and embrace the experience at hand rather than withdrawing from it. This is how you accumulate knowledge to be deposited in your wisdom well that can change your life.

- Do you ever find yourself making the same mistake repeatedly like my dog, Mac? It's important to remember that you are activating the law of attraction every time you fail to learn from a previous experience that inflicted pain or suffering on yourself. In a manner of speaking, you are placing an order with the Universe for more of the same.

- Do you believe it is possible to be "nourished" by every experience you have, including the painful ones? How did Joseph Campbell's statement, "The Universe always strikes you at your weakest point because that's what most needs strengthening," feel when you first read it? The practice is to remember that when you take lessons the Universe offers personally, you circumvent your own growth.

- Can you see that the wisdom of remaining teachable applies to your life regardless of where you are on your journey? This practice applies even after you have achieved the consciousness to live an authentic life. If you remain teachable, there will continue to be (re)defining moments opening in front of you, inviting you to pause and look directly into the face of the Beloved, only to be reminded that who you *really* are is the Beloved looking at Itself.

CHAPTER 15

Mindfulness Is the Practice; Purpose Points the Way

Becoming Who You Were Born to Be Is the Gift You Have Come to Share

The best and safest thing is to keep a balance in your life,
acknowledge the great powers around us and in us. If you can
do that, and live that way, you are really a wise man.

—EURIPIDES

Hopefully, after having read the previous fourteen chapters, you can now more readily discern those moments when you become so mesmerized by what is happening on the surface of life, you forget about the amazing true Self lying at the center of your being. My intention throughout has been to offer encouragement not to linger too long either on the surface or at the center because we need both to have an authentic, balanced, and meaningful life. The question is, how much of our authentic self will we remember to bring to the surface as our body goes about its daily business? In this final chapter, we are going to explore why finding the balance between the two is so crucial, not only for ourselves but also for the world in which we live.

Beyond the What, Who, When, Where, and How, Is the *Why*

"I want to remind us all that the world is listening, all the time. How we are ripples out from us into the world and affects others. We have a responsibility—an ability to respond—to the world. Finding our particular way of living this responsibility, of offering who we are to the world, is why we are here."

—Oriah Mountain Dreamer

At the onset of our journey together, I suggested that you might consider this book a seeker's guide to living an authentic life and that it is in your (re)defining moments you are guided back to your ancient roots, the Original Self from which you came. It is there that your authentic self, an individuated spark from an eternal flame, will be found. In prior chapters, we discussed the importance of (re)defining moments and the "what, who, when, where, and how-to"s of living as an authentic being. But the question that deserves one last pass is the "why." What is the real point of living an authentic life? Why bother fine-tuning your awareness and ability to discern your (re)defining moments when they occur? Why bother becoming who you were born to be? Why does living mindfully and authentically from the center of your being while *on the surface of life* really matter?

The Sacred Sojourn

The answer to these questions can be found in the wisdom teachings of the ages. Throughout history, great masters and avatars have taught the meaning and importance of the sacred sojourn—a devotional act of "retreating" from the world to reflect, remember, and reconnect with "something" larger than themselves referenced in chapter 1. This sojourn was accomplished by ascending to the highest mountaintop, far above the din and confusion of the lowlands, where the masters would sit in silence, contemplate, and connect to their ancient roots of oneness with the Original Self, the Light from which they knew they emanated as divine sparks. This was their time to be reminded of the importance of living life from the inside out. For them, these were (re)defining moments because they washed away the layers of forgetfulness endemic of the people in the lowlands who lived chronically, and unknowingly, with spiritual amnesia. This respite on the mountaintop was a gift they gave themselves because it enabled them to mindfully open the portal to the Self, to look deeply into themselves and see and remember the authentic being they truly were. Equally important, however, it offered them an opportunity to see and appreciate the most precious gift of all: Life itself and how it was encoded in their soul to be uniquely expressed, unlike any other human being on the planet. While one's purpose for being on the planet may be *realized* on the mountaintop, it is never fulfilled there. It must be *actualized* in daily life. Thus, therein lies the answer to "why" living mindfully and authentically really matters to us and our world: the masters knew the most important part of their sojourn was coming back down the mountain. They knew they were not meant to remain there.

The word *sojourn* means "to stay somewhere temporarily." The masters understood that the purpose of their life was not to withdraw from the world and blissfully hang out on the mountaintop. They knew that to honor the giver of Life required them to bring the richness and uniqueness of the gift they found within back down the mountain and into everyday life and share it with others who had forgotten that they also were *each* a critically important and unique part of "something" infinitely larger than themselves. The masters knew it was their task to awaken others to the reality that there was more to life than just enduring day to day until they exited the planet, that there was a divine endowment of unique purpose and meaning awaiting each of them if they only made the sojourn themselves. They also knew it was not just their words that would awaken others; it was the manner in which they shared their gift, how they lived their lives with authenticity, courage, transparency, and reverence.

Activating the Authentic Self

Your purpose, beyond actualizing your authentic self, awaits you in the process of your unfolding. It will never be found simply by scaling the pyramid of the hierarchy of your own personal needs. Being who you are matters; the gift of your authentic self is the gift you have come to share with the world.

The story of the masters ascending to the mountaintop is also our story. At the end of the day, if we are to live an authentic life in a manner that impacts the world in life-affirming ways, we know we must each make the sacred sojourn. The good news is, you don't have to retreat to a distant mountaintop for the experience. If you were to directly invert the pathway of the ancient one's retreat to the mountaintop, you'd see that you, too, can make the sacred sojourn by simply taking the vertical plunge *below* the surface of life to the deepest part of your innermost being. However, from that place you *must* return to the surface, like the rising sun that spreads its radiance each morning, benefiting all living things each new day. Realizing the precious gift of Life and how it has been *uniquely* encoded in you is what activates your authentic self. At the end of day, the timeless message the masters bring to us is that living authentically from the center of your being matters because the world needs that which only *you* can bring to life.

The Gift Is Not Found Only in What You Do with Your Life, but *How* You Do It

This is often the juncture at which our minds begin to scramble, perhaps experiencing a bit of panic trying to discern just what our gift might "look like." Just stop! Take a deep breath, go to the mirror, and you'll see the gift, *the entire gift,* gazing back at you. Because you are a recipient of Life, *you* are the gift in a very uniquely wrapped package sent here to be shared with the world. You are one of a kind, and it is when you live out loud from the center of your being that you literally become the delivery system for the authentic self. This, then, is your purpose—to bring your authentic self to the party called your life, to be who you were born to be. Your (re)defining moments are those divinely planned portals that help you actualize your purpose. The practice, however, is to remember that it's not only "what" you do in the world that matters, it's *how* you do it; it's the mindfulness and the sense of authenticity with which you do whatever is yours do. In this regard, every human being's *purpose* is the same—to bring the deepest part of themselves to the surface and unabashedly share it with the world. The manner in which each one personalizes the gift is their *mission*—and because there are no two people on the planet alike, nor shall their missions be the same. Your individualized mission is found in whatever you are called to do that honors the giver of the gift in a manner that integrates your authentic self with the doing self. If you take time to consider this thought, you'll recognize that every moment of every day is an open portal through which you can bring the unique gift of yourself to every encounter. The practice is to remember that the operative words are *every encounter.*

This Is the Moment

"Life can be found only in the present moment. The past is gone, the future is not yet here, and if we do not go back to ourselves in the present moment, we cannot be in touch with life."

—THICH NHAT HANH

As I said at the beginning of this book, while it is the road less traveled, the pathway to living an authentic life is lined with one defining, enriching moment after another. So again I ask, what *if* you were to reconfigure your concept of "a" defining moment and elongate it? What *if* you could be so mindful on your pilgrimage that your life becomes a sacred continuum, a series of (re)defining moments, each one seamlessly linked, taking you deeper—below "surface living"—allowing you to see more clearly the authentic self you truly are and have always been? What *if* you were to successfully access that authentic part of yourself that finds its ancient roots in that "something larger than you" and mindfully bring it to the surface, into your life today and every day? Can you imagine yourself living your life from the inside out, so courageously, so transparently, so authentically that who you really are shows up in every sacred moment? These are all questions worth exploring because, if approached consciously, mindfully, and gently, they will lead you back to an awareness that the gift that has been given to you is beyond value and it awaits your full acceptance. After all, what is a gift if never opened or used?

It's Not about Where You Have Been or Where You Are Going—It's about Where You Are *Now*

"What lies behind us and what lies ahead of us are tiny matters compared to what lives within us."
—HENRY DAVID THOREAU

To give you a visual example of what life as a sacred continuum looks like, consider the image on the following page. Consider the horizontal line as the "business" of your life—your "doing" whatever it is you do that moves forward from left to right, linearly, moment-to-moment, hour-to-hour, and day-to-day on the surface of life. Think of the vertical line that intersects with the horizontal line as your "being," which, in the context of this book, can be defined as both a noun and a verb. Consider any

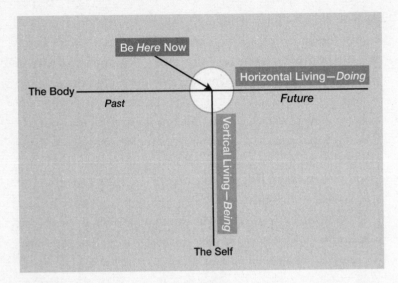

point on the horizontal line to the left of the vertical line as the past and anything to the right, the future. I've drawn a small circle around the point where the two lines intersect; inside this circle represents the present moment, where your "being" merges with your "doing." To consciously live inside that small circle is called the practice of mindfulness.

To merge your being with your doing is a sacred practice of witnessing your soul-self—that part of your authentic self that knows it is on a mission and that it is one with the infinite Presence from which it came, vertically ascending from the depths to the center of the circle as it moves along the horizontal pathway of your life. In this context, mindfulness represents the conscious awareness that you are more than the experience at hand on the surface of life. With mindfulness, we remember that while we must live on the surface of life and exist in a human skin, the presence of the One is always with us, every moment, one step, one breath, one sacred second at a time. Living closer to the center of our being is the practice of a lifetime, but so, too, is skillfully living on the horizontal plane—the surface of life— where our purpose for being on the planet is uniquely expressed.

You Have a Right to Be Here, and You Have a Right to Be Yourself

"Go placidly amid the noise and haste, and remember what peace there may be in silence . . . Speak your truth quietly and clearly . . . If you compare yourself with others, you may become vain and bitter . . . Be yourself . . . Beyond a wholesome discipline, be gentle with yourself. You are a child of the universe, no less than the trees and the stars; you have a right to be here. And whether or not it is clear to you, no doubt the universe is unfolding as it should . . . whatever your labors and aspirations, in the noisy confusion of life, keep peace in your soul. Be cheerful. Strive to be happy."

—MAX EHRMANN, FROM "DESIDERATA"

You are here on this planet at this time because you are supposed to be here; *this* is your time. You are here by divine appointment. Just as it can take tens of thousands of years for the light of a distant star to reach the earth, the *what* you are arrived on the planet to become the *who* you are at precisely the right moment. You are a divine idea whose time has come to shine, born of the Universe. Everything herein was intended to bring you to *this* precise moment, a moment in which you see deeply into the truth of *what* you are and *who* you are and to remember that they are one and the same. Living an authentic life is probably the most challenging thing a human being can endeavor to undertake because it is not the way of the world, but it is the way of the heart that connects you to what is real, what is meaningful, and what is eternal.

Have you arrived at a point where you feel at home in your life? Are you comfortable in your own skin? Have you made peace with yourself and the world around you? Do you sense that you are part of something far greater than what you can see in the mirror? These are all questions that only your heart can answer because it is directly connected with the ancient roots of the Original Self, that infinite Presence that breathed the breath of Life into *you*. That is how important you are to the Universe. Imagine how worthy you must be to have been given such a precious gift. Acknowledge the gift of who you truly are, and share it with others joyfully. And be gentle with yourself as you begin your own pilgrimage. Infinite (re)defining moments lie ahead, and many of them have *your* name deeply inscribed on them, just awaiting your arrival with open arms.

Now, breathe, smile, and embrace the fact that you really are a child of an infinite Universe expanding at the speed of light. You are on the most amazing journey of becoming who *you* were born to be. How beautiful is that?

Peace,
Dennis

Recommended Reading

Adyashanti. *Falling into Grace*. Boulder, CO: Sounds True, 2011.

Bach, Richard. *Illusions*. New York: Delacorte Press, 1977.

Barks, Coleman. *The Essential Rumi*. New York: Quality Paperback Book Club, 1995.

Beckwith, Michael Bernard. *Spiritual Liberation*. New York: Atria Books, 2009.

Campbell, Joseph. *The Power of Myth*. New York: Anchor, 1988.

Carter-Scott, Cherie. *If Life Is a Game, These Are the Rules*. New York: Broadway Books, 1998.

Chopra, Deepak. *The Seven Spiritual Laws of Success*. New York: Amber-Allen, 1994.

Coelho, Paulo. *The Pilgrimage*. New York: HarperOne, 2008.

Dass, Ram. *Polishing the Mirror*. Boulder, CO: 2013.

Elgin, Duane. *The Living Universe*. San Francisco, CA: Berrett-Koehler, 2009.

De Mello, Anthony. *Awareness*. New York: Doubleday, 1990.

———. *The Way to Love*. New York: Doubleday, 1991.

Dyer, Wayne. *Change Your Thoughts—Change Your Life*. New York: Hay House, 2009 (reprint edition).

Gibran, Kahlil. *The Prophet*. New York: Alfred A. Knopf, 1977.

Hanh, Thich Nhat. *The Heart of the Buddha's Teaching*. New York: Broadway Books, 1998.

———. *Peace Is Every Step*. New York: Bantam Books, 1998.

———. *Your True Home*. Boston, MA: Shambhala, 1998.

Hendricks, Gay. *The Big Leap*. New York: HarperOne, 2009.

Holmes, Ernest. *The Science of Mind.* New York: G. P. Putnam's Sons, 1938.

———. *This Thing Called You.* New York: Tarcher/Penguin, 2004.

Jampolsky, Gerald G. *Forgiveness.* Hillsborough, OR: Beyond Words Publishing, 1999.

Jones, Dennis Merritt. *The Art of Being: 101 Ways to Practice Purpose in Your Life.* New York: Tarcher/Penguin, 2008.

———. *The Art of Uncertainty: How to Live in the Mystery of Life and Love It.* New York: Tarcher/Penguin, 2011.

———. *How to Speak Science of Mind.* Camarillo, CA: DeVorss, 2010.

Kornfield, Jack. *The Art of Forgiveness, Lovingkindness, and Peace.* New York: Bantam Books, 2002.

LaRue, Ronda. *Remembering Who You Really Are.* Lincoln, NE: iUniverse, 2003.

Levoy, Gregg. *Callings.* New York: Three Rivers Press, 1997.

Lipton, Bruce. *The Biology of Belief.* Santa Rosa, CA: Mountain of Love/Elite Books, 2005.

Oriah. *The Call, Reprint Edition.* New York: HarperOne, 2006.

———. *The Invitation, Reprint Edition.* New York: HarperOne, 2006.

Pauch, Randy. *The Last Lecture.* New York: Hyperion, 2008.

Pressfield, Steven. *The War of Art.* New York: Grand Central Publishing, 2002.

Ruiz, Don Miguel. *The Four Agreements.* San Rafael, CA: Amber-Allen, 1997.

Singer, Michael A. *The Untethered Soul.* Oakland, CA: New Harbinger, 2007.

Studna, Carl. *Click!* Los Angeles, CA: Agape Media International, 2012.

Tolle, Eckhart. *A New Earth.* New York: Dutton/Penguin, 2006.

———. *Stillness Speaks.* Novato: New World Library, 2003.

Zinn-Kabot, Jon. *Wherever You Go, There You Are.* New York: Hyperion, 1999.

Zukav, Gary. *The Seat of the Soul.* New York: Fireside, 1989.

———. *Soul to Soul.* New York: Free Press, 2007.

———. *Spiritual Partnership.* New York: HarperOne, 2010.

Zukav, Gary, and Linda Francis. *The Heart of the Soul.* New York: Simon & Schuster, 2001.

Acknowledgments

It is with great respect and gratitude that I acknowledge those who have supported me in bringing this book to fruition: first, to my business partner, Diane—who also just happens to be my best friend, playmate, travel companion, and wife—for being my second set of eyes and doing the preliminary edit of this book. Her insights, suggestions, and patience helped me keep it all together during the creative process. I also thank her for graciously creating the spaciousness in our relationship that allowed me to take the time to honor the divine nudge when this book was ready to be given birth. To my dog, MacDoodle, the mystical superpoodle, for his vigilance in laying under my desk and keeping my feet warm, my heart open, and my mind present in the moment . . . and for reminding me when it was time to call it a day. To my publisher, Joel Fotinos at Tarcher/Penguin, for continuing to believe in me, mentor me, and remind me of my potential to go deeper, and then giving me the space to do so. To my prayer partners, Dr. Sue Rubin, Dr. Patrick Cameron, and Rev. Cynthia James, for continuing to remind me who I truly am in those moments when I forget. To my friends and peers in the New Thought Spiritual Community, especially those affiliated with the Centers for Spiritual Living. Unity Centers, and AGNT (the Association for Global New Thought) located throughout the United States, Canada, and the world.

To the many great minds I quote throughout this book who have inspired me with their wisdom, both ancient and current. And most important, to the Original Self, who is the real creator of this book. With humility and boundless love, I say thank you all.

About the Author

Throughout his lifetime, Dennis Merritt Jones has been on a quest to inspire and lift people to a higher expression of life. His personal vision is to guide people to their purpose, knowing that when a person fully awakens to who they are and why they are on the planet, they begin to naturally share their gift with humankind and, in the process, create an enriching life for themselves and the world around them.

Dennis is the author of the award-winning books *The Art of Uncertainty: How to Live in the Mystery of Life and Love It* and *The Art of Being: 101 Ways to Practice Purpose in Your Life*, both released by Tarcher/Penguin, and *How to Speak Science of Mind*, published by DeVorss and Company. He is also a columnist for *The Huffington Post* and various print media as well as a consultant and spiritual mentor to organizations and individuals in many parts of the world.

Dennis believes we each have the capacity and, ultimately, the responsibility to contribute something positive to this world, leaving it a better place than it was when we arrived—concepts reflected in his writings and seminars. He uses his understanding of universal principles to draw upon wisdom from both Eastern and Western philosophies. Dennis believes that the consciousness of unity, cooperation, and reverence for life and the planet will be one of the most significant influences upon society as we approach the challenges and uncertainties of twenty-first-century living.

CONTACT INFORMATION:

Please visit www.DennisMerrittJones.com or write to:

PO Box 940837

Simi Valley, CA 93094-0837.

E-mail: info@dennismerrittjones.com